STUDIES IN ORIENTAL RELIGIONS

Edited by Walther Heissig and Hans-Joachim Klimkeit

Volume 18

PHILIP C. ALMOND

HERETIC AND HERO

Muhammad and the Victorians

1989

OTTO HARRASSOWITZ · WIESBADEN

PHILIP C. ALMOND

HERETIC AND HERO

Muhammad and the Victorians

1989
OTTO HARRASSOWITZ · WIESBADEN

The series STUDIES IN ORIENTAL RELIGIONS is supported by

Institute of Comparative Religion
Bonn University

Institute of Central Asian Studies
Bonn University

in collaboration with

Institute for Advanced Studies
of World Religions New York

Institute of History of Religion
Uppsala University

Donner Institute, Academy of Åbo
Åbo, Finland

Institute of Oriental Religions
Sophia University, Tokyo

Department of Religion
University of Hawaii

CIP-Titelaufnahme der Deutschen Bibliothek

Almond, Philip C.:
Heretic and hero : Muhammad and the Victorians / Philipp C.
Almond. – Wiesbaden : Harrassowitz, 1989
(Studies in oriental religions ; Vol. 18)
ISBN 3-447-02913-7
NE: GT

© Otto Harrassowitz, Wiesbaden 1989
Das Werk einschließlich aller seiner Teile ist urheberrechtlich geschützt. Jede Verwertung außerhalb des Urheberrechtsgesetzes bedarf der Zustimmung des Verlages. Das gilt insbesondere für Vervielfältigungen jeder Art, Übersetzungen, Mikroverfilmungen und für die Einspeicherung in elektronische Systeme.
Satz: Satz-Offizin Hümmer, 8702 Waldbüttelbrunn
Otto Harrassowitz, Kreuzberger Ring 7c-d, 65205 Wiesbaden,
produktsicherheit.verlag@harrassowitz.de
Sigel: StOR

ISSN 0340-6792

For my parents
TENNYSON K. AND ELLIE

Table of Contents

Acknowledgements IX

Prologue 1

Chapter One: Heretic and Hero 3
                1. Changing Images 3
                2. Muhammad and Satan 7
                3. The Imposter 10
                4. The Deluded Enthusiast 16
                5. Muhammad's Sincerity 18
                6. Muhammad as an Epileptic 20
                7. From Mecca to Medina 28
                8. Muhammad the Prophet? 31

Chapter Two: Portraits of the Prophet 33
                1. Ambition and Lust 33
                2. Muhammad and the Sword 35
                3. Predestination and Fatalism 41
                4. Pleasures and Paradise 44
                5. Muhammad and the Miraculous 49
                6. The Night Journey 53
                7. The Profligate Prophet? 56

Chapter Three: The Prophet and the Book 65
                1. The Conspiracy and the Book 65
                2. The Prophetic Potpourri 70
                3. The Religion of the Book 78
                4. Islam and Culture 81
                5. The Noble Arab? 88

Epilogue	95
Bibliography	97
Index	105

Acknowledgements

Although much has been written on nineteenth century British religious thought, little attention has thus far been paid to Victorian attitudes to non-Christian religions. This study, the second in a series devoted to this issue, hopes to fill a lacuna in studies about Victorian images of Muhammad and Islam.

I should like to acknowledge my indebtedness to two scholars in particular: to Edward Said whose analysis of Orientalism stimulated my research both in an earlier work on Buddhism and in this study of Islam; and to Norman Daniel whose magisterial works on Islam and the West remain of enormous value to any research into Western images of Islam. I am grateful too to the staffs of the University of Queensland Library and The British Library for their unfailing helpfulness. Special thanks are due to Ms. Roni Hawkins who typed the manuscript.

Prologue

Muhammad the Prophet was born around A.D. 570 at Mecca. He came from a family which might once have been powerful but whose influence had lessened. He married a wealthy widow, Khadija, for whom he had worked as a camel driver. Around A.D. 610, he received his first revelation from God through the archangel Gabriel. Some three years later he began his public teaching. He recited to his contemporaries that which had been revealed to him by God. The collection of these texts constitutes the Quran, which for Muslims is quite simply the word of God.

The situation at Mecca having become quite untenable for him, he emigrated in A.D. 622 to Medina with a handful of followers. This event, the Hijra, marks the beginning of the Muslim era. At Medina, Muhammad established the Islamic community and became the ruler of the city. In A.D. 630, the Meccans signed a treaty with Muhammad and he trimphantly re-entered the city which had become the ritual focus of the religion of Islam. He died in A.D. 632. Twenty years after his death, an Arabian empire reached from Iran to Libya. A hundred years later, it extended from India and the borders of China to the south of France. Since that time, for the Christian West, Islam has remained often threatening, sometimes enchanting, but ever present. The self-image of the West was constructed on a foundation in which Islam was essentially other.

This book is concerned with one aspect of the Western image of Islam, specifically the portrayal of Muhammad and the religion he founded, in nineteenth century England. The period is a particularly crucial one in Western understandings of Islam. For it was a time when traditional images of Muhammad as a heretic were juxtaposed with new images of Muhammad as hero, when Muhammad the Antichrist confronted Muhammad the noblest of Arabs.

In part, as we shall see, the proliferation of images of Muhammad in both the eighteenth and nineteenth centuries was the result of a burgeoning of Western knowledge about Muhammad and the origins of Islam during these centuries, and particularly during the Victorian period. Undoubtedly, historical-critical Western scholarship played a significant role in the subtle interplay of "fact" and interpretation which created for the West the various meanings of Islam, of its origins, its founder, and its developments. Moreover, such scholarly work not only influenced but was influenced by the abundance of popular literature about Muhammad and Islam in the nineteenth century, literature as crucial, if not more so, for our understanding of the meaning of Islam for the Victorians, and of the Victorians' understanding of themselves. Whether in scholarly discourse or in popular polemic, the facts about Muhammad and Islam were, so to say, merely the warp and woof of the screen upon which the image of this religion was projected.

This work, then, stands in the tradition notably established by Edward Said in his *Orientalism*. Like Said, I am primarily concerned with the internal structure of Western views of Islam and its origins, apart from the question of how Islam "really" was. However, this study of the Victorians and Islam differs from that of Said in several ways. First, in contrast to Said's methodological emphasis on the unity of Orientalist discourse, this work emphasises the plurality of approaches to Islam, and stresses the discord in images of Muhammed. Thus, discourse about Islam is much richer, more diverse, and more complex than Said has demonstrated. Second, in contrast to Said's concentration on discourse about nineteenth and twentieth century Islam, this work focuses on discussions of Muhammad and the origins of Islam. This will enable us to discern the often subtle relationship that existed within discourse about Islam between the principles and practices of the traditions, and between the pure original and its latterday manifestations.

CHAPTER ONE

Heretic and Hero

1. Changing Images

> A silent great soul; he was one of those who cannot *but* be in earnest; whom Nature herself has appointed to be sincere. While others walk in formulas and hearsays, contented enough to dwell there, this man could not screen himself in formulas; he was alone with his own soul and the reality of things. The great Mystery of Existence ... glared-in upon him, with its terrors, with its splendours; no hearsays could hide that unspeakable fact "Here am I!" Such *sincerity*, as we named it, has in very truth something of divine. The word of such a man is a voice direct from Nature's own Heart.[1]

On Friday, May 8, 1840 Thomas Carlyle addressed an audience of politicians, philosophers, men of letters, and clerics. His subject was the Hero as Prophet, his exemplar Muhammad. His audience found it powerful if bewildering, although Carlyle himself thought it the best lecture he had ever given.[2] Influenced by Goethe's *West-Eastern Divan*, by Herder's and Friedrich Schlegel's perspectives on Islam, puzzled by the Quran but inspired by the *Arabian Nights*, Carlyle found in the inner experience of the Arabian prophet that quintessential quality of his Great Men – sincerity.[3]

Carlyle's image of the Prophet as hero was both cause and effect of a significant change in attitudes to Islam and its founder during both the eighteenth and nineteenth centuries in the West. His image of Muhammad was one of many which reflected a radical shift in attitudes which gained increasing momentum during the eighteenth and particularly the nineteenth centuries. And it created a new image of the Prophet which permeated the Victorian understanding of Islam.

However, although a more sympathetic understanding of Muhammad dominated the Victorian period, more ancient images persisted. A demonic imposter continued to offset an heroic and valiant Muhammad in the literature of the Victorian period. For many, a more balanced picture was deemed desirable. In 1858, for example, the *National Review* criticised not only those who regarded Muhammad as a cold and scheming imposter inspired by Satan, but also those

---

1 Carlyle, *On Heroes*, p. 54.
2 See Kaplan, *Carlyle*, p. 265.
3 On Carlyle and Muhammad, see especially Watt, "Carlyle on Muhammad;" and Nash, "Thomas Carlyle and Islam."

whose admiration for Muhammad was just as partial and unmerited. And it called for a full, fair, and free inquiry so that a clear, unbiased, and unambiguous verdict could be reached.[4]

Such a verdict would have been unlikely for a number of reasons. First, it is clear that for some writers an admiration of Muhammad did not entail an endorsement of Islam. Edward Freeman in *The History and Conquest of the Saracens* was impressed by Carlyle's image of the Prophet; and he endorsed the propensity of the modern liberal spirit to recognize greatness and goodness in the heroes of alien systems. But he rejected the view that Islam was a tradition wholly worthy of admiration, and could not endorse the taking up of the Muslim cause merely because of political alliances with the Turks against Russia:

> Mahomet, the legislator and reformer of Arabia, I venture to revere along with the legislators and reformers of other lands. But Mahometanism, seated on the ruins of Christianity and civilization, I can only regard as an object of abhorrence ... So far from my wish to do justice to Mahomet arising from any sympathy with existing Mahometanism, my real and heartfelt admiration for the ancient Arab does not even lead me to look with the slightest complacency upon the modern Turk.[5]

Moreover, in the nineteenth centy, Islam continued to provide grist for the mills of anti-Christian polemic and intra-Christian conflict. *The Christian Remembrancer* for 1855 lamented the fact that the panegyrists of Islam employed it as a weapon aimed at the decay and ultimate overthrow of Christianity. This was an exaggeration, but it does indicate that some Christians were concerned that Islam was now an enemy within the walls as well as without. A concerted assault on Christianity by a unified fifth column of Islamic sympathisers was unlikely. As *The Christian Remembrancer* itself recognised, there was a variety of images of Islam in the essays, treatises, biographies, and histories "in which Mahometanism is successively portrayed as it appeared to spectators who have gazed upon it with the glance of a philosopher, a sceptic, a latitudinarian, an ultra-Protestant or a Roman Catholic divine."[6] Still, a number of Christian writers felt that the pendulum had swung too far in favour of Muhammad. And there was alarm among the more conservative representatives of Prostestant missionary endeavour. For S. W. Koelle, for instance, a member of the Church Missionary Society and one of the late Victorian period's most vehement critics of Muhammad and Islam, the more toler-

---

4 *National Review*, 1858, pp. 137–8.
5 Freeman, *History and Conquest of the Saracens* p. 39.
6 *The Christian Remembrancer*, 1855, p. 88; see also *Dublin University Magazine*, 1876, p. 133.

ant attitude was merely evidence of the tyranny of fashions. Indeed, he claimed, "So strong has the modern fashion of justice to Mohammad grown, that it has sometimes manifested itself by positive misstatements in his favour."[7]

Fashion or not, what Koelle and others had correctly perceived was that traditional Christian images of the Prophet and Islam were, in the Victorian period, no longer dominant. Without putting too fine a point on it, it was the development of a more secular view of history from the eighteenth century onwards, and the progressive decline of Christian "sacred history" which made possible shifts in attitudes to Muhammad and his religion. This change in the criteria upon which such assessments were made was recognised at the time. As early as 1833, John Roebuck in his *Life of Mahomet* remarked, "We have now almost universally ceased to regard our own faith as at all concerned in the estimation that may be formed of the character, opinion, conduct, or religion of Mahomet."[8]

As we shall see later, Roebuck was overstating the case. But broadly speaking, discussions of Muhammad and Islam, and assessments both positive and negative, tended during the Victorian period to be based, not on biblical or theological grounds but on historical-critical principles. As Ernst Renan pointed out, Washington Irving's *The Life of Mahomet* in 1850, although not demonstrating a very elevated historical sentiment, "shows a true progress when we consider that in 1829 Mr. Charles Forster published two large volumes (very much relished by the clergy) in order to establish that Mahomet was nothing but the Little Horn of the he-goat which figures in the 8th chapter of Daniel, and that the Pope was the Great Horn."[9] Matthew Arnold was later to bemoan, in the light of Renan's critique, the absence in England of any force of educated literary and scientific opinion which would make impossible the aberrations of amateurs like Charles Forster.[10] And it was the case that England lagged behind both France and Germany in the development of both Oriental studies and philology.[11] Nevertheless, Forster's was the last major attempt in nineteenth century England to interpret Islam from the perspective of a Christian apocalyptic history.

However, it would be quite improper to suggest that Christian authors, *qua* Christians, were implacably opposed to reinterpretations of Islam. On the contrary, they were often in the vanguard of the Western re-habilitation of Muhammad. For example, Frederick D. Maurice, the Anglican divine, in his influential *The Religions of the World* saw Muhammad, not merely as a hero, but as

---

7 Koelle, *Mohammed and Mohammedanism*, pp. vii–viii.
8 Roebuck, *Life of Mahomet*, p. 12.
9 Renan, *Studies*, p. 156.
10 Arnold, *Essays*, pp. 59–60.
11 See e.g., Said, *The World, The Text, and the Critic*, ch. 12.

the instrument of the divine: "It was a mercy of God that such a witness, however bare of other supporting principles, however surrounded by confusions, should have been borne to his Name, when His creatures were ready, practically, to forget it."[12]

Conversely, those who professed to approach Muhammad and Islam on historical-critical grounds did not always arrive at a sympathetic conclusion. John Roebuck, for example, was committed to the principles of secular historical inquiry, but his conclusions differed little from those of traditional Christian anti-Muslim polemic. Mohammad remained for him "a barbarian unskilled in the sciences of which he professed himself the inspired teacher..."[13]

Still, in spite of the co-existence of earlier images of Muhammad with more recent ones, there was undoubtedly a fundamental shift in images of Islam between 1700 and 1900, and one that accelerated during the early Victorian period. As early as 1846, *The Prospective Review* noticed that such a change had taken place: "The same persons, perhaps, who might have been able to form a reasonable and tolerant view of Zoroaster or Buddha, have no mercy for one who declared that he came not to destroy the law or the gospel, but to reclaim both to their monotheistic foundations. The tendency to this latter extreme, however, seems now, happily, to belong to the past."[14] Twenty-five years later, *The Quarterly Review* reflected on a century and a half of Western images of the Prophet:

> How the silly curses of the Prideaux, and Spanheims, and D'Herbelots; how their "wicked impostors" and "darstardly liars" and "devils incarnate", and Behemoths and beasts and Korahs and six hundred and sixty-sixes gave room, step by step almost, to more temperate protests, more civil names, less outrageous misrepresentations of both the faith and the man: until Goethe and Carlyle, on the one hand, and that modern phalanx of investigators ... Sprenger, and Amari, and Nöldeke, and Muir, and Dozy, on the other, have taught the world at large that Mohammedanism is a thing of vitality, fraught with a thousand fruitful germs; and that Mohammed, whatever view of his character ... be held, has earned a place in the golden book of Humanity.[15]

In the Romantic individualism of Carlyle, the heretic had become a hero; in the criticism of secular historians, the myth had become history.

---

12 Maurice, *The Religions of the World*, p. 24.
13 Roebuck, *Life of Mahomet*, p. 31.
14 *The Prospective Review*, 1846, p. 164.

2. Muhammad and Satan

> The smoke of the infernal cave
> Which half the Christian world o'erspread,
> Disperse, thou heavenly light, and save
> the souls by that imposter led –
> That Arab thief, as Satan bold,
> Who quite destroyed thy Asian fold.
>
> Oh may thy blood once sprinkled cry,
> For those who spurn thy sprinkled blood!
> Assert thy glorious Deity,
> Stretch out thine arm, thou triune God!
> the Unitarian fiend expel,
> And chase his doctrine back to hell.
>
> Charles Wesley
> "For the Turks"

Charles Wesley, like many of his eighteenth century contemporaries was convinced that Muhammad was a satanically inspired imposter. In so believing, he was reflecting, in part, the medieval view of the intimate relationship between Muhammad, Satan, and the Anti-christ. As Jacques de Vitry had put it in the thirteenth century, "... like another Antichrist and the first-born son of Satan, transfigured like Satan into an angel of light, Muhammad, upheld by God's great anger and special displeasure, with co-operation of the human race, perverted ... more people than any other heretic before his time."[16]

The imaginative vision of Muhammad as Anti-christ was to continue, albeit in a progressively attenuated form, until at least the beginning of the twentieth century. It was supported by interpretations of Muhammad's name. In 1665, for example, Thomas Herbert simply declared that Muhammad's name in Arabic signified deceit, "affording also the number 666, the mark of Antichrist."[17] Occasionally, it was disputed. In his popular *Pansebeia*, first published in 1653, Alexander Ross gave ten reasons why Muhammad could not have been the Anti-christ. He claimed, for example, that the Anti-christ would be a Jew of the tribe of Dan, and not an Arabian descended from Ismael and Hagar.[18] Still, apocalyptic imagery did pre-

---

16 Daniel, *Islam and the West*, p. 185.
17 Herbert, *Some Years Travels*, p. 336.
18 Ross, *Pansebeia*, p. 165.

dominate. The name "Mahomet," he concluded, "is signified by death, which rideth on the Pale Horse."[19] Such apocalyptic imagery appeared also in his *A Needful Caveat or Admonition*, which was appended to the first English translation of the Quran in 1649, itself a translation of the French version by du Ryer: "The Star which fell from Heaven and opened the bottomless pit ... meant *Mahomet* that great destroyer, as his name signifieth, answering to the name *Apollyon*, and *Abaddon*."[20] Moreover, he declared, Muhammad was "that little Horn which did spring up among the ten Horns of the great and terrible Beast of the *Roman Empire*."[21]

Such apocalyptic interpretations of Islam did not play a major role in the eighteenth or nineteenth centuries. But, as I have already indicated, the discourse of apocalypticism resurfaced with some vigor in the Reverend Charles Forster's *Mahometanism Unveiled* in 1829. Although Forster saw Islam as a pioneer for Christian evangelism, because Muhammad travestied the characters of Moses and Christ and presented himself to the Jews as their messiah, "he established incontrovertibly his providential office, as the predicted antichrist of the East."[22] But Forster's Providential theory of history was generally not enthusiastically received. In its review of *Mahometanism Unveiled*, *The Edinburgh Review* showed just how outmoded such apocalypticism had become. "Religious subjects, or secular subjects religiously discussed," it declared, "cannot be left to the elaborate travesty of a learned masquerade, however perfect the good faith with which it may be put on ... Many who might dress the Ark of Israel with gracious garlands, and serve to dance before it, may yet be very unfit champions to lead it into gratuitous battles of their own provoking, or to defend it by the prowess of their single arm."[23] Muhammad was named the Anti-christ by de Lacy Johnstone as late as 1901 in his popular and un-critical *Muhammad and His Power*; and the pseudonymous author of a virulent tirade against Islam in 1903 assured his readers that Muhammad was undoubtedly one of the predicted Anti-christs.[24] But such statements read as the linguistic vestiges of a world chronology no longer culturally viable. Satan and secular history were incompatible.

This can be clearly seen in critical reactions to one of the most important products of Victorian scholarship on Islam, Sir William Muir's *The Life of Mahomet*, first published in 1861. Unlike Forster, Muir's hermeneutical framework was

19 *Ibid.*, p. 119.
20 du Ryer, *The Alcoran of Mahomet*, p. ix.
21 *Ibid.*, p. ix.
22 Forster, *Mahometanism Unveiled*, i. 282.
23 *The Edinburgh Review*, 1829–30, p. 289.
24 See Johnstone, *Muhammad and His Power*, p. 159; Amos, *The New but True Life*, p. 65.

not that of a providential view of history. On the contrary, Muir's study was essentially historical-critical. But there were theological aspects to Muir's work which, for some of its reviewers, had uneasily and inappropriately superimposed themselves on Muir's historical method. The *British Quarterly Review* in 1872, for example, expressed a common conviction that secular and theological history should not be mixed: "When Sir William Muir hints his belief that in some parts of his career Mahomet was the subject of what we may call a Satanic inspiration, he is putting forth a view which he has a perfect right to maintain as a theological proposition, but he is treading on ground whither the historian of events and creeds must refuse to follow him."[25]

Muir's Satanic intimations were at odds with most of the major nineteenth century accounts of Islam, both in England and on the Continent, which proceeded on the assumption that Islam could only be interpreted naturalistically. And Muir was criticized by Continental scholars. To Jules Barthélemy St.-Hilaire, in ascribing the actions of Muhammad in Medina to Satanic inspiration, Muir had done Muhammad an almost complete injustice.[26] Aloys Sprenger perceived more clearly the methodological reasons for this. He wrote, "As the geologists manage to explain the revolutions of our planet by natural powers known to us, so also, I believe, the origin of Islam is capable of explanation in a quite natural way, and we do not need to ascribe to the Devil an influence upon it, nor to other powers, which have ceased to be active in our time."[27]

British images of Muhammad as Anti-christ were influenced too by Reformation accounts of both Muhammad and the Pope as joint Anti-christs, of the East on the one hand, and the West on the other.[28] In 1652, for example, Peter Heylyn in his *Cosmographie* observed that "*Mahomet* compiled his devilish doctrine, beginning his Empire; and Boniface the third assumed his *Anticristian* title, beginning his unlimited Supremacy, nigh about the same year."[29] Most importantly, the theory gained wide circulation through its inclusion in a work which was to remain a standard source for British interpretations of Islam for the next two hundred years. this was Humphrey Prideaux's *The True Nature of Imposture Fully Displayed in the Life of Mahomet*, first published in 1697. According to Prideaux,

> *Mahomet* began this Imposture about the same time that the *Bishop* of *Rome*, by virtue of a grant from the wicked Tyrant *Phocas*, first as-

---

25 *British Quarterly Review*, 1872, p. 107; see also Smith, *Mohammed and Mohammedanism*, p. 98.
26 Barthélemy St.-Hilaire, *Mahomet et le Coran*, p. 114.
27 Sprenger, *Das Leben*, i. xi.
28 On the attitude of the Protestant Reformers to Islam, see Williams, "Erasmus and the Reformers."
29 Heylyn, *Cosmographie*, p. 123.

sumed the Title of *Universal Pastor* ... And from this time Both having conspired to found themselves an *Empire* in *Imposture*, their Followers have been ever since endeavouring by the same Methods, that is, those of Fire and Sword, to propagate it among Mankind; so that *Antichrist* seems at this time to have set both his Feet upon *Christendom* together, the one in the *East*, and the other in the *West* ...[30]

A century later, the issue was still considered worthy of discussion. In 1799, for example, the anonymous author of a life of Muhammad spent several pages arguing, on the basis of the Muslim calendar, that the two events could not have both occurred in the same year, A. D. 606.[31] But most writers on Islam in the nineteenth century did not feel obliged to defend *or* attack Prideaux's account of dual Anti-christs. To be sure, in a number of popular accounts of Islam in the 1820's, Prideaux's words, although unacknowledged, remained part of anti-Muslim and, one might add, of anti-Catholic apologetic.[32] And as late as 1859, the Reverend G. Akehurst of London, declared in a short pamphlet entitled *Imposture Instanced in the Life of Mahomet* that both Muhammad and the Bishop of Rome "conspired to found themselves an empire in imposture, by means of fire and sword, so that Anti-Christ at that period seems to have set both his feet upon Christendom together – the one in the East and the other in the West ..."[33] In effect, however, by the middle of the nineteenth century, such discourse was passé, and in the general framework of mid to late Victorian discussions of Muhammad has somewhat an air of quaint antediluvianism.

3. The Imposter

The case was otherwise with that most central of issues in discussions of Muhammad – the question of imposture. This was an issue which had not only played a decisive part in medieval and early modern theologically motivated accounts, but would remain central in later historical-critical studies.

At the end of the seventeenth century. There appeared three works which, in

30 Prideaux, *The True Nature of Imposture*, p. 16.
31 Anon, *The Life of Mahomet*, 1799, pp. 18–20.
32 See e. g., anon., *The History of Mahomet*, 1821, p. 9; Williamson, *Reflections on the Four Principal Religions*, i. 129.
33 Akehurst, *Imposture Instanced*, p. 9.

their attitudes to Muhammad, typified Western images of the Prophet in the middle of the so-called Age of Reason. One of these was Pierre Bayle's *Dictionnaire historique et critique*. Bayle was concerned to argue against the notion that Muhammad was sincerely deluded by the devil into the belief that he was a prophet. For Bayle, a naturalistic explanation was to be preferred. Muhammad was an imposter: "his insinuating behaviour, and dexterous address, in procuring friends, very plainly shew, that he made use of religion only as an expedient to aggrandize himself."[34] Bayle's account is interesting for several reasons. On the one hand, it is an early example of the shift from theological to naturalistic accounts of Islam that gathered pace in the following two centuries. But on the other hand, it is a clear indication that there was to be no necessary correlation between naturalistic or historical accounts of Muhammad and sympathetic responses to him.

The imaginative congruity of "Muhammad" and "imposture" was further reinforced in 1697 in d'Herbelot's *Bibliothèque orientale*, the first systematic attempt to make the Orient a coherent part of the intellectual furniture of the West. As Edward Said writes, "what may have been a loose collection of randomly acquired facts concerning vaguely Levantine history, Biblical imagery, Islamic culture, place names, and so on were transformed into a rational Oriental panorama from A to Z."[35] Muhammad was categorised as the Imposter. Under the entry for Mahomet, we read, "this is the famous imposter Mahomet, Author and Founder of a heresy, which has taken on the name of a religion that we call Mahometan."[36] "The imposter" was to remain the "scientific" way of discriminating the Prophet from other Muslims of the same name in encyclopaedic entries until the early part of the Victorian period. It occurred, for example, in *The English Encyclopaedia* in 1802, the *Pantologia* in 1813, the *Encyclopaedia Perthensis* in 1816, and in the *Encyclopaedia Britannica* in 1817 and 1823.[37] That it did not occur in most Victorian encyclopaedias is some evidence of the fact that, by the middle of the nineteenth century, a changing image was in the air.

Most influential of all was Prideaux's *The Nature of Imposture Fully Displayed*. Prideaux's work was a pastiche of elements drawn secondhand from Arabic sources and from anti-Muslim Christian polemic. But the life of Muhammad was nonetheless constructed on an historical framework, although very traditional images of Muhammad and Islam were imposed upon it. Muhammad remained the imposter. According to Prideaux, "betaking himself to frame such a *Religion* as he thought

---

34 Bayle, *Historical and Critical Dictionary*, ii. 250.
35 Said, *Orientalism*, p. 65.
36 D'Herbelot, *Bibliothèque orientale*, ii. 648.
37 *The English Encyclopaedia*, 1802, v. 466; *Pantologia*, 1813, vii. 142; *Encyclopaedia Perthensis*, xiii. 571; *Encyclopaedia Britannica*, 1817, xii. 401; *Encyclopaedia Britannica*, 1823, xii. 401.

might best go down with them, he drew up a *Scheme* of that *Imposture* he afterwards deluded them with, which being a Medley made up of *Judaism*, the several *Heresies* of the *Christians* then in the *East*, and the old *Pagan* Rites of the *Arabs*, with an indulgence to all Sensual Delights, it did too well answer his Design in drawing men of all sorts to the embracing of it."[38]

That many, even of Prideaux's contemporaries, were puzzled by his unhappy blending of the historical and the polemical is clear. In 1720, for example, the pseudonymous Abdulla Mahumed Omar in his "A Defence of Mahomet" applauded Prideaux for confuting the false accounts of most of his predecessors; yet, he wondered why there remained "so much rancour drest up in abundance of Falshood..."[39] And the author of *Reflections on Mohammedism* in 1735, recognising that no passions were more violent than those aroused by the mention of Muhammad and his law, questioned Prideaux's ambivalent attitude to the Prophet. "How comes it," he asked, "that it is, with the Multitude, thought a Crime to speak a word in his Favour, while others are applauded to the Skies, who fall short of him in everything desirable in a Man?"[40]

In part at least the ambivalence thus perceived was the result of Prideaux's apologetic concerns, in particular the Deist and Socinian sympathy for Islamic monotheism against which he was writing.

But such concerns were no longer relevant to his nineteenth century readers, and by the middle of the nineteenth century his judgement of Muhammad was more often condemned than supported. Historical data had rendered suspect some of Prideaux's conclusions. More importantly, attitudes had changed. As *The Eclectic Magazine* asserted in 1858, "The *Life of Mahomet* by Humphrey Prideaux... may, without hesitation, be pronounced a marvellous specimen of unconscious blindness and perverted reasoning."[41]

However that may be, Prideaux's blending of traditional images of Islam and an historical framework had many imitators in the eighteenth and nineteenth centuries. The author of an anonymous life of Muhammad in 1712 stressed the great pains he had taken in presenting Muhammad in the most just, natural, and lively way, and in viewing him in the same way Muslims considered him. "I thought it but fair," he insisted, "to follow the Accounts of the *Arabian* Authors themselves, rather than the Fictions of those who esteem'd it a Merit to invent all the Calumnys they could, in order to discredit both *Mahomet* and his Religion."[42] Laudable aims, on the face

38 Prideaux, *The True Nature of Imposture*, p. 13.
39 *Miscellanea Aurea*, p. 166.
40 Anon., *Reflections on Mohammedism*, 1735, p. 6–7.
41 *The Eclectic Magazine*, 1858, p. 456; see also *National Review*, 1858, p. 139.
42 Anon., "The Life and Actions of Mahomet, extracted chiefly from Mahometan Authors," in *Four Treatises*, p. 6.

of it. But, as he went on to suggest, the original sources themselves would be sufficient "to expose this Deceiver, and his Reveries, to the Laughter and Contempt of all the sensible part of Mankind."⁴³ History, like myth, could serve the same polemical ends.

The same must be said of Joseph White's account of Muhammad in his *Sermons Preached Before the University of Oxford in the Year 1784*. As Archbishop Laud's Professor of Arabic, his scholarship was undeniable; and, during the course of his work, he cited the major Arabists of the preceding two centuries – Edward Pococke, George Sale, d'Herbelot, J. H. Hottinger, Adrian Reland, Ludovico Marracci, and of course Prideaux. White's aim was to be objective about Muhammad. He did not wish to admit "either the undistinguishing censures of his exasperated opposers, or the exaggerated encomiums of his infatuated adherents."⁴⁴ For his account of the life of Muhammad, White followed the text of Abu'l-Fida on the Prophet's life published by Jean Gagnier at Oxford in 1723.⁴⁵ This Arabic text, accompanied by a Latin translation, was to remain the major Arabic source for the life of Muhammad until the middle of the nineteenth century.⁴⁶ White's major source then was respectable, although as one of the later lives of Muhammad, not impeccable. But White's evaluation of the Prophet remained the traditional one of the imposter: "among all the instances of audacious and successful imposture, which history has recorded, none has been more widely diffused, or more firmly established, than that of the pretended prophet of Arabia."⁴⁷

As with Prideaux, so also with White, the uneasy combination of historical method with the endorsement of Muhammad's imposture did not go unremarked. The most perceptive criticism was offered by Godfrey Higgins in 1829. Higgins's aim was expressly to increase a brotherly feeling towards Muslims, although his own partiality to the kind of anti-Christian polemic he found so objectionable in Christian anti-Muslim apologetic was not calculated to endear him to his Christian readers. Still, he did suggest why in White, anti-Muslim sentiment co-existed with putatively historical scholarship. Of White, he wrote, "Since the general exemplary life of the prophet could not be denied by the learned Oxonian, but as his merit could not be admitted without danger by a Christian divine, nothing remained but

---

43 *Ibid.*, p. 6.
44 White, *Sermons*, p. 87.
45 Gagnier, *Ismael Abu'l-Feda*.
46 Muir's account in his *Life of Mahomet* of the sources for the life of Muhammad indicates the burgeoning number of traditional Arabic sources available to the Victorian scholar. See Muir, *The Life of Mohammad*, ch. 1.
47 White, *Sermons*, p. 31.

to attribute the conduct of the prophet to hypocrisy, and the most artful and deeply laid plot and design."[48]

The combination of the historical and the image of imposture remained a feature of a number of popular anonymously written lives of Muhammad until the middle of the nineteenth century. In a 1799 life of Muhammad, Prideaux, Hottinger, and Pococke were utilised to support the claim that "any country might blush to have produced such a monster."[49] A sixpenny pamphlet in 1815, *Life and Actions of Mahomet, the Famous Oriental Imposter*, followed Abu'l-Fida's life to establish its case.[50] The life of Muhammad published by the Religious Tract Society in 1847 was an extremely vitriolic attack on Muhammad and Islam, although it used Prideaux, Boulainvilliers, Gagnier, Sale, Hottinger, and Gibbon to support its claim to tell the story of the Prophet "with a conscientious regard to what is believed to be the truth."[51] And the 1851 life of Muhammad published by the American Mission Press, while purporting to be a sober, matter-of-fact history nonetheless concluded that Muhammad was "decidedly the most successful imposter that ever lived."[52]

Surprisingly, far from the much more detailed knowledge about Muhammad and Islam functioning to destroy the image of the imposter, paradoxically it often enhanced it. For some, the image of Muhammad as the imposter was just too ingrained. Robert Beverley, for example, in his reply to Higgins's *Apology* in 1829 considered the religion of Muhammad "ably explained by Sale" and its early history "beautifully narrated by Gibbon." But, he went on to argue, "those who would prove that Mohammed was no imposter, are, to use the words of Rabelais, 'shearing donkeys to get wool.'"[53] For others, the new historical image of Muhammad as a man of asceticism and sobriety was all the more evidence of his duplicity and disingenuousness. Thus, for example, according to William Sime in 1837, Muhammad, in order to effect his scheme for palming a new religion, "affected a more than ordinary degree of sanctity, affected to pass his time in religious retirement and meditation; and became more grave in his deportment and more profuse in his charity..."[54]

For many, the new knowledge about the life of Muhammad resulted in, if not the denial of his imposture, at least a different attitude towards it. For Henri Boulainvilliers, the author of the eighteenth century's most sympathetic account of Islam,

---

48 Higgins, *An Apology*, p. 9.
49 Anon., *The Life of Mahomet*, 1799, p. 2.
50 Anon., *Life and Actions of Mahomet*, 1815.
51 Anon., *The Life of Mohammed*, 1847.
52 Anon., *Life of Mohammad*, 1851.
53 Beverley, *A Letter to Godfrey Higgins*, p. 56.
54 Sime, *History of Mohammed*, p. 17.

Muhammad remained an imposter. But he was nonetheless worthy of esteem. "*Mahomet*, the imposter," he wrote,

> was neither coarse nor barbarous; ... he conducted his enterprize with all the art, all the delicacy, all the resolution, all the intrepidity, and extensive views that *Alexander* or *Caesar* had been capable of, in his circumstances... he knew less than those two heroes, of avarice, interest, luxury, and prodigality... He did not more enslave his country; on the contrary, he only desir'd to govern it, in order to make it the mistress of the world, and its various riches; of which, both he, and his first successors made so disinterested a use, that in this respect they much compel the admiration of their greatest enemies.[55]

The logic implicit in Boulainvilliers' argument became clear four years later in the anonymous *Reflections on Mohammedism*. Its author was uncertain whether Muhammad was an imposter. But even if so, he began his imposture "deeming it perhaps no Crime to deceive Men into their own Good."[56] A century later, *The Encyclopaedia Britannica* inclined to the same view: "if he cannot be freed from the reproach of having deceived men by attributing to himself a divine mission which he had not received, it may perhaps be conceded that the end which he contemplated gives to his imposture a character less odious than would otherwise belong to it."[57] And *The North British Review* in 1855, although it still regarded Muhammad as an imposter, could not deny "that his theory contains much that is true in theory and excellent in practice."[58]

But for many commentators of the early and mid Victorian periods, the historical evidence was quite simply incompatible with the image of Muhammad as imposter. Carlyle's position was common, if more vividly expressed than was usual: "for a wretched Simulacrum, a hungry Imposter without eyes or heart, practising for a mess of pottage such blasphemous swindlery, forgery of celestial documents, continual high-treason against his Maker and Self, we will not and cannot take him."[59] To Johann Moehler, if Muhammad were a common deceiver, both his moral character and his asceticism would have been inexplicable. More inexplicable still would have been the Quran in which Moehler found "quite an original piety, a touching devotion, and a peculiar religious poetry."[60]

---

55 Boulainvilliers, *The Life of Mahomet*, p. 244.
56 Anon., *Reflections on Mohammedism*, 1735, p. 8.
57 *The Encyclopaedia Britannica*, 1842, xiv. 31.
58 *The North British Review*, 1855, p. 456.
59 Carlyle, *On Heroes*, p. 67; see also pp. 43–4.
60 Moehler, *On the Relation of Islam*, p. 23; see also pp. 20–2.

4. The Deluded Enthusiast

If the image of Muhammad generated by analysis of the Muslim sources was not obviously compatible with the discourse of imposture, there remained other images which did more easily square with the evidence. One was that of Muhammad as a deluded fanatic and religious enthusiast. For some at least, Muhammad was both imposter and enthusiast, the latter as reprehensible as the former, and more socially threatening. To the author of a life of Muhammad in 1712, he was primarily the imposter; but he was also comparable with the Quakers and the Camisards: "Those Tremblings, Quakings, Tossings of the Head and Limbs, which we read *Mahomet* was subject to, may well be supposed to have been just such Convulsions, Agitations and fanatical Throws as have seiz'd many Enthusiasts..."[61]

There were other more subtle attempts to discriminate between enthusiasm and imposture. As early as 1655, the Anglican Meric Casaubon had applied an empirical method to the analysis of religious enthusiasm, with a view to discerning true inspiration from fraudulent imposture. Muhammad, in his view, was an enthusiast, but he was not certain he was an imposter. "We are commonly told," he remarked, "that *Mahomet* did assume to himself divine authority by feigned Enthusiasmes. By false, we are sure enough as to Divine Authority: but whether feigned, I make some question..."[62]

The issue of imposture versus enthusiasm was still an alive one in 1734, the year in which George Sale published his translation of the Quran. Sale assumed that Muhammad was an imposter. But he was determined to be fair in his assessment of both Muhammad and the Quran. "I have thought myself obliged," he wrote, "to treat both with common decency, and even to approve such particulars as seemed to me to deserve approbation: for how criminal soever Mohammad may have been in imposing a false religion on mankind, the praises due to his real virtues ought not to be denied him."[63] But it is clear that Sale is very concerned to avoid the imputation of enthusiasm to Muhammad, and the implication of fanaticism that it carried in the Restoration period. As Addison had suggested in the *Spectator* in 1711, enthusiasm was a weakness of human reason which made mankind lower than the beasts. Thus, for Sale, better the wise, virtuous imposter than the irrational enthusiast:

> it is easy to conceive that he might think it a meritorious work to rescue

---

61 Anon., "The Life and Actions of Mahomet, extracted chiefly from Mahometan Authors," in *Four Treatises*, p. 29. On the Camisards, or French Prophets, who arrived in England around 1710, see Knox, *Enthusiasm*, ch. 15.
62 Casaubon, *A Treatise*, p. 11.
63 Sale, *The Koran*, p. vii.

The Deluded Enthusiast 17

the world from such ignorance and superstition; and, by degrees, with the help of a warm imagination which an Arab seldom wants, to suppose himself destined by Providence for the effecting of that great reformation. And this fancy of his might take still deeper root in his mind during the solitude he thereupon affected... One thing which may probably be urged against the enthusiasm of this prophet of the Arabs, is the wise conduct and great prudence he all along showed in pursuing his design, which seem inconsistent with the wild notions of a hot-brained religionist.[64]

In the later part of the eighteenth century, and into the nineteenth, religious enthusiasm no longer carried the radical political and social implications it had held in Commonwealth and Restoration times. Enthusiasm was more often viewed as potentially self-deceptive than socially destructive. The deluded enthusiast was no longer necessarily a fanatic. As Nathan Alcock put it in 1796, "Enthusiasm may cause a man to deceive himself, and take his own fancies and conceptions for divine suggestions. This probably was the case with Mahomet and the success of his enterprizes might still further persuade him that his cause was the cause of God."[65] For H.H. Cludius too, writing in the context of German Pietism, and more especially Romanticism, Muhammad was not so much a deceiver as an enthusiast (ein Schwärmer) who was deceived.[66]

To be sure, the image of Muhammad as an enthused fanatic still occurred in the early part of the nineteenth century. Charles Mills, for example, in his *An History of Muhammedanism* maintained that Muhammad's entry into public life was that of a wild and clamorous fanatic. The prophet preached the unity of the Godhead "with all the incoherence, and with all the assumption of authority from the Almighty, which distinguishes fanatics of every religion."[67] But, unlike Muhammad's, Mills's voice was crying in the wilderness.

As the developing historical awareness of Muhammad had rendered the image of the imposter difficult to sustain, so also did it make unfeasible that of the fanatic, and the identification of Muhammad with the excesses of European religious enthusiasm. A clear case in point is Vans Kennedy's "Remarks on the Character of Muhammad," published in 1823. He argued that, except in affirming that he received revelations from heaven Muhammad never acted in a way different from the rest of mankind. Moreover, he maintained, a sincere belief in, and a firm adherence to such revelations should not be called enthusiasm. It was by no means

64 *Ibid.*, p. 30.
65 Alcock, *The Rise of Mahomet*, p. 30–1.
66 Cludius, *Muhammeds Religion*, p. 27.
67 Mills, *An History*, p. 37; see also pp. 11–12.

necessary, he continued, "that a person who fancies himself inspired by Heaven should be divested of human prudence, or that he should act as if he were under the influence of phrensy."[68] Even more difficult to understand, to Kennedy, was the charge of fanaticism. Never was a purer religion propagated than that of Muhammad, he declared, and never one which more inculcated charity and benevolence among its followers.[69]

For *The Penny Cyclopaedia* in 1839, the Prophet was a quiet man, a perfect model of Arabian virtue, brave and liberal, eloquent and vigorous, noble and simple in all his dealings, and of irreproachable morality. The language of enthusiasm is still invoked, but it is no longer decisive in the assessment of Muhammad. On the contrary, rather than functioning to criticise the Prophet, it serves to excuse such fraud, cruelty, and injustice as were present in the first propagation of Islam. "A religious enthusiast," we read, "is compelled to act according to the overpowering suggestions of his imagination, which he easily persuades himself to be the inspirations of Heaven, and according to his own conviction of the importance and justice of his mission."[70]

By the middle of the nineteenth century, to be labelled an enthusiast was no longer a reproach. The image of Muhammad as an enthusiast, sincere if deluded, received very picturesque expression in Washington Irving's *Life of Mahomet* in 1850. To Irving, Muhammad's enthusiasm was a means to noble ends. "There is something striking and sublime," he wrote, "in the luminous path which his enthusiastic spirit struck out for itself through the bewildering maze of adverse faiths and wild traditions; the pure and spiritual worship of the one true God, which he sought to substitute for the blind idolatry of his childhood."[71]

5. Muhammad's Sincerity

Irvings's *Life of Mahomet* was much criticised for its romantic approach to Muhammad and Islam, and for its lack of historical rigour. *The Eclectic Magazine*, for example, described it in 1850 as elegant but jejune; and it declared that it was not the sort of life of the Prophet "as ought by this time to have been laid before the

---

68 Kennedy, "Remarks," p. 429.
69 *Ibid.*, p. 429; see also pp. 417, 424, and 426–7.
70 *The Penny Cyclopaedia*, 1833, p. 302.
71 Irving, *Life of Mahomet*, p. 236.

English public."[72] And William Muir criticised it for too often losing sight of the truth "amid the charms of a romantic style and an enchanting narrative."[73]

Such criticisms of Irving's work were in part justified, particularly when we compare it with the work upon which it was based, namely, Gustav Weil's *Mohammed der Prophet* published some seven years previously. But Irving's account undoubtedly struck a sympathetic chord, one that had been sounded ten years earlier by Carlyle, and one that corresponded to the mood of the times. As *The Eclectic Magazine*, in its review of Irving, put it, "We do not suppose that there is any person of culture now living that would be inclined to revive the old hypothesis of deceit and imposture. That hypothesis, against which Mr. Carlyle so valiantly did battle, has now no longer any professed existence amongst us..."[74]

This was, perhaps, an overstatement. Still, by the mid Victorian period, the predominant image of the Prophet was, without doubt, that of the sincere, if mistaken, hero. *The Encyclopaedia Britannica* aptly summarised the position in 1858:

> On the whole, looking at the natural workings of an ardent imagination, exalted by meditation and solitude at a time when his countrymen were in an unsettled religious state; the conviction wrought upon those nearest to him...; his endurance for twelve years of every species of insult and persecution; his steady rejection of every offer of wealth and chieftainship, made on the condition of desisting from his endeavours; the simplicity of his mode of life to the very last; - we cannot accept the views of Voltaire, or of Prideaux and Marracci, but must so far side with Möhler, Caussin, Carlyle, Irving, and others, as to believe in the general sincerity of Mohammed, and his faith in himself and his own mission. [75]

Such views remained common for the remainder of the Victorian period. In 1865, for instance, Barthélemy Saint-Hilaire maintained there were no more reasons to doubt the sincerity of Muhammad's belief in his divine mission, than that of Socrates.[76] The Harrow schoolmaster, R. Bosworth Smith, the mid-Victorian period's most influential defender of the Prophet, argued that there was no single trait in Muhammad's character during his Meccan period which could imply imposture. On the contrary, he maintained, "there is everything to prove the real

---

72 *The Eclectic Magazine*, 1850, p. 52.
73 Muir, *The Mohammedan Controversy*, p. 69.
74 *The Eclectic Magazine*, 1850, p. 47; see also *The Christian Remembrancer*, 1855, p. 109.
75 *The Encyclopaedia Britannica*, 1853–60, xv. 301.
76 Barthélemy Saint-Hilaire, *Mahomet et le Coran*, p 101.

enthusiast arriving slowly and painfully at what he believed to be the truth."[77] In 1877, *Harper's New Monthly Magazine* simply declared, of the Meccan period, that there could be no doubt of Muhammad's sincerity.[78] W. Quartermaine East in his *The Last Days of Great Men* in 1903 followed Muir, Smith, and Carlyle. For him both Muhammad and Oliver Cromwell were alike in their earnestness and sadness, their self-reprobation and self-sought salvation, and in considering virtue alone as estimable for itself.[79]

By the end of the nineteenth century then, the sincerity of Muhammad was the generally accepted presupposition upon which discussion of his life and teachings proceeded. Much to his chagrin, that most vehement of late Victorian critics, S. W. Koelle, was forced to admit it, albeit with a typical theological gloss: "error becomes all the more dangerous a masterpiece of Satan the better it succeeds in assuming the semblance of Truth or mixes itself up with it; and the more its advocates uphold it with an air of sincerity and earnestness."[80]

6. Muhammad as an Epileptic

> By the Star when it plunges,
> your Comrade is not astray, neither errs,
> nor speaks he out of caprice.
> This is naught but a revelation revealed,
> taught him by one terrible in power,
> very strong; he stood poised,
> being on the higher horizon,
> then drew near and suspended hung,
> two bows'-length away, or nearer,
> then revealed to his servant that he revealed.
>
> Quran 53.1–10
>
> Your companion is not possessed;
> he truly saw him on the clear horizon;
> he is not niggardly of the Unseen.
>
> Quran 81.22–4

---

77 Smith, *Mohammed and Mohammedanism*, p. 108.
78 *Harper's*, 1877, p. 405.
79 East, *The Last Days*, p. 306. The nineteenth century had rehabilitated Cromwell too. Compare Addison, *The Life and Death of Mahumed*, p. 35 in 1679 in which both Muhammad and Cromwell are imposters.
80 Koelle, *Mohammed and Mohammedanism*, p. 69.

> Did we not expand thy breast for thee
> and lift from thee thy burden?
>
> Quran 94.1–2

The shifts in attitudes to Muhammad that we have been examining may be further illuminated by reference to Western interpretations of the Prophet's putative epilepsy. The Western accounts of Muhammad as an epileptic were imposed, in part, upon the biographical traditions of the Prophet, in part upon a number of passages in the Quran. Suras 53 and 81, for example, inform us that a heavenly messenger appeared to him. In a series of later inspirations, as Muhammad believed, the archangel Gabriel communicated to him the words of God. And Muhammad's experience of God's purification of him through the opening of his breast, as recounted in Sura 94.1–2, was much embellished in the Muslim biographies. Angels are said to have split open his abdomen and to have removed a black clot of blood.[81]

The Muslim tradition accepts that, during his inspired states, Muhammad's behaviour was not normal. Indeed, it counted as evidence of his prophetic status. But from a very early period in the history of Christian reaction to Islam, Muhammad's experiences were interpreted as symptomatic of epilepsy. Most importantly, the diagnosis of epilepsy was married to the image of fraud and imposture. The diagnosis of Muhammad as an epileptic probably originated in Christian Byzantium. Less than two hundred years after the death of Muhammad, the Byzantine historian Theophanes explained the origin of Islam in this way:

> He had an epileptic seizure, and when his wife noticed this she became very distressed, for she was noble and had now been joined to a man who was not only helpless but epileptic as well. He turned to conciliating her, saying, "I see a vision of the angel known as Gabriel, and faint and fall because I cannot bear up under the sight of him." She had a friend living there who was a monk exiled for false belief, and she told him everything, even the angel's name. He wanted to reassure her, and told her, "He has spoken the truth, for this angel is sent to all the prophets. She was the first to accept the false abbot's statement; she believed in Mohammed, and told other women of her tribe that he was a prophet.[82]

This story of Muhammad's dissembling to his wife had an extremely wide circulation in the medieval West, especially as a result of its inclusion in Vincent of

---

81 See Schimmel, *And Muhammad is his Messenger*, pp. 67–8.
82 Turtledove, *The Chronicle*, p. 35.

Beauvais's *Speculum Historiale*.[83] We find it, for example, in the *Travels* of John Mandeville in the mid-fourteenth century, in one of the most popular histories during the fourteenth and fifteenth centuries – Higden's *Polychronicon*, and in the mid-sixteenth century *Cosmographye* of Sebastian Muenster.[84] It appeared also in William Lithgow's *A Most Delectable and True Discourse* in 1614,[85] and in Joseph Wybarne's *New Age of Old Names* in 1609. Wybarne's account, although having a more negative attitude to Muhammad's wife (and women in general) demonstrates nonetheless an essential continuity with the Byzantine story. According to Wybarne, when Khadija rebuked him,

> as if he were a drunken beggar, he meaning that she should publish what he sayed, intreated her to conceale it: for as a River stopped, grows higher above the bankes, so there is a generation called Women, which being desired to be silent, will tell it more liberally; he told her then to this effect: Have you not read that *Daniel* was sicke when he saw the Angel? It is the Angel *Gabriel* which appearing to me, thus astonisheth my senses.[86]

Most importantly, the attention of all English readers of the Quran was drawn to the story as a result of its inclusion in the first English translation of the Quran in 1649.[87]

It is perhaps surprising that there seems to have been no reference to Muhammad inventing his revelations to excuse his epilepsy in order to appease his wife after this date. But the general notion of Muhammad simulating revelations to justify his epileptic seizures remained common. Humphrey Prideaux, for instance, gave just such a general version: "And whereas he was subject to the *Falling-Sickness*, whenever the Fit was upon him, he pretended it to be a *Trance*, and that then the *Angel Gabriel* was come from *God* with some new *Revelations* unto him..."[88]

This more general version of the story had also appeared in the early Western sources. Here, for example, is Lydgate's account from around 1440. Muhammad, we read,

> In his excuse seide that Gabriel
> Was sent to hym from the heuenli mansioun
> Be the Hooli Goost to his instruccioun:

---

83 See Vincent, *Speculum Historiale*, xxiii. ch. xl.
84 See Letts, *Mandeville's Travels*, i. 99–100; Babington, *Polychronicon*, p. 39; and Muenster, *Cosmographye*, p. 63.
85 Lithgow, *A Most Delectable and True Discourse*.
86 Wybarne, *The New Age*, p. 94.
87 See du Ryer, *The Alcoran*, p. 398.
88 Prideaux, *The True Nature of Imposture*, p. 20.

> For the aungel shewed hym so sheene,
> To stonde upricht he myhte not susteene.[89]

The same story was repeated in the various editions of George Sandys' *Travailes*, in *The Life and Death of Mahomet* in 1637 attributed to Sir Walter Raleigh, and in Peter Heylyn's *Cosmographie* in 1652.[90] William Biddulph in 1609 had a different version again. According to this story, Muhammad, as the leader of a band of robbers, was loathed by his confederates for his epilepsy. He therefore, Biddulph went on, "to redeem himself from this contempt pretended a divinitie in his doings, faining himself to enter communication with God...."[91]

As early as the 1670's, the notion of epilepsy was rejected by Henry Stubbe in his exceptionally – for its time – sympathetic view of the prophet.[92] It is difficult to gauge the influence of Stubbe's work, for it was circulated only in manuscript form, although it is likely that Prideaux knew it and was concerned to negate its positive image of Muhammad. In the eighteenth century however, the ascription of epilepsy was dismissed by both Gagnier and Sale.[93] Edward Gibbon in his *The History of the Decline and Fall of the Roman Empire*, fully aware of its Byzantine origins, described it as "an absurd calumny of the Greeks,"[94] and saw it as merely an example of gross bigotry.

But the combination of epilepsy with imposture remained during the nineteenth century, despite the denials of Gagnier, Sale, and Gibbon. In 1821, for instance, in an anonymous life of Muhammad composed for popular consumption, we are told that whenever he had an epileptic attack, "he pretended it was a trance, and that then the angel *Gabriel* came from *God* with some new revelations unto him, the splendour of whose appearance he not being able to bear, this caused him to fall into those trances, in which the angel conversed with him..."[95] Even as late as 1905, David Margoliouth, Laud's Professor of Arabic at Oxford from 1888, suggested that, as a result of his experience of epilepsy, Muhammad was able to simulate epileptic fits to give credibility to his revelations[96]; and Menezes, a priest of Mangalore writing for his "dear friends and countrymen, the Mahommedans of

---

89 Quoted by Smith, *Islam in English Literature*, p. 6.
90 See Sandys, *Travailes*, p. 42; Raleigh, *The Life and Death of Mahomet*; and Heylyn, *Cosmographie*, p. 121.
91 Biddulph, *The Travels*, p. 50.
92 See Stubbe, *An Account*, pp. 81–2, 149.
93 See Gagnier, *Ismael Abu'l-Feda*, p. 9; and Sale, *The Koran*, p. 466.
94 Gibbon, *Decline and Fall*, iii. 160.
95 Anon., *The History of Mahomet*, 1821, p. 12; see also anon., *The Life of Mahomet*, 1799, p. 131.
96 See Margoliouth, *Mohammed*, pp. 85–6.

India,"⁹⁷ informed his readers that, although Muhammad's first revelations may have been hysterical hallucinations, he subsequently made "use of this natural infirmity with great sagacity to convince people that at such times he was favoured with heavenly inspirations and revelations from God."⁹⁸

Thus, between Prideaux in 1698 and Menezes in 1911, union of the images of Muhammad as an epileptic and Muhammad as an imposter was a constant. But interestingly, the relationship between the two had changed. For Prideaux and those before him, the revelations were invented by Muhammad to excuse his epilepsy. For Margolioth and Menezes the epileptic seizures were simulated to justify his revelations. How, then, is such a change in the relationship of epilepsy and imposture to be explained?

The clue lies in Menezes's reference to "hysterical hallucinations." For it indicates that the issue of the relationship between Muhammad's supposed epilepsy and his revelations was intimately connected to nineteenth century diagnoses of epilepsy, and most importantly, analyses of the relation between epileptic seizures and religious states. And as Owsei Temkin remarks, "the medical evaluations of Mohammed rested heavily on the interpreter's religious and philosophical orientation, as well as on the nosological fashions of the day, and not just on the material on hand."⁹⁹

It was Gustav Weil, in 1843, in his *Mohammed der Prophet*, who signalled an alternative understanding of the relationship between Muhammad's epilepsy and his revelations. Weil combined the traditional image of Muhammad as an epileptic with a conviction of his sincerity. According to Weil, Muhammad had rationally come to the conclusion that he was a prophet of God, and his epileptic fantasies reinforced this belief. No-one will doubt, he claimed, "that, for the greatest part, Mohammed's visions occurred in association with epileptic fits. However, unlike Theophanes, I do not believe that he put forward the appearance of Gabriel in order to conceal his illness, but that, on the contrary, he was himself induced by this malady to believe in it."¹⁰⁰

Weil's theory was made familiar to English readers by a note in Irving's *Life of Mahomet* in 1850.¹⁰¹ But it had been brought to their attention in a review of Weil's book in *The Prospective Review* some four years earlier. With Gibbon clearly in mind, the reviewer declared that it was no longer questionable that what had once been seen as a calumny against Muhammad was now proved: Muhammad was an

---

97 Menezes, *The Life and Religion of Mahomet*, p. 183.
98 *Ibid.*, pp. 20–1.
99 Temkin, *The Falling Sickness*, p. 372.
100 Weil, *Mohammed der Prophet*, pp. 44–5, n. 48.
101 See Irving, *Life of Mahomet*, ch. vi. note.

epileptic. However, crucially, he went on to make the point that, for Weil, Muhammad did not feign the appearances of the angel Gabriel as a screen for his malady; rather it, was "his paroxysms which induced him to believe in those appearances himself."[102]

Particularly as a result of Weil's work, the image of Muhammad as a deluded epileptic became part of Victorian discourse about the Prophet. Though G. Latham Browne in his biography of Muhammad in 1856 was inclined to the view that the growth of his power was the result of his craft, skill, and guile, he nonetheless did suggest that epilepsy may well have deranged the mind of Muhammad.[103] *The Quarterly Review* in 1869 admitted that Muhammad was an epileptic but refused to accept this as an explanation for the success of his mission, or of his religious inspiration: "We ... do not think that epilepsy ever made a man appear a prophet to himself, or even to the people of the East; or, for the matter of that, inspired him with the like heartmoving words and glorious pictures."[104] But in the same journal eight years later, Muhammad's belief in his prophetic call was seen as the result of his epileptic fits.[105] And *The Dublin Review* in 1878 was of the opinion that Muhammad was the unfortunate victim of his own delusions.[106]

The image of Muhammad as a deceived epileptic was common in much general literature. Stanley Lane-Poole for instance, in his popular *Studies in a Mosque*, in 1883 saw the ultimate cause of Muhammad's call to prophesy as the result of a finely-constituted and nervous nature created by cataleptic fits which had occurred in Muhammad's childhood. "Given this nervous nature," he wrote, "and the grim solitude of the hill where he had wandered for long weary months, blindly feeling after some truth upon which to rest his soul, it is not difficult to believe the tradition of the cave that Mohammed heard a voice say, 'Cry!'"[107] Winwood Reade in his widely read work on Islam in Africa, *The Martyrdom of Man*, first published in 1872, saw him as the victim of his own delusions.[108] Weil's theory even influenced British medical discussions of epilepsy. James Howden in the *Journal of Mental Science* in 1873, citing Weil, declared, "There is strong evidence that Mahomed was an epileptic, and that, though a man of undoubted power and strong religious

---

[102] The *Prospective Review*, 1846, p. 167; see also *The Encyclopaedia Britannica*, 1858, xv. 3000: "He had always been subject to fits of epilepsy. this was long supposed to be a Christian calumny by Gibbon and others; but the researches of Weil have proved its truth."

[103] See Browne, *Biography*, pp. 127–8.

[104] *The Quarterly Review*, 1869, p. 311.

[105] See *The Quarterly Review*, 1877, pp. 215–6.

[106] See *The Dublin Review*, 1878, p. 403.

[107] Lane-Poole, *Studies*, p. 42.

[108] See Reade, *The Martyrdom of Man*, pp. 259–60.

feeling, he founded his pretensions as a medium of revelation on visions which appeared to him during epileptic trances."[109]

Apart from Weil, the most important influence on Victorian discussions of Muhammad's mental and physical health was Aloys Sprenger. In 1851, in a little known life of Muhammad published in India by the Presbyterian Mission Press, Sprenger had suggested that, after Muhammad assumed his prophetic role, he was subject to paroxysms of cataleptic insanity which progressively assumed more of an epileptic character. Although he recognised that such an affliction was often accompanied by psychological phenomena, the overall image presented of Muhammad is that of an imposter.[110]

However, by the 1860's, both his diagnosis and his interpretation have changed somewhat. In his *Das Leben und die Lehre des Mohammed*, he argued that, since Muhammad did not suffer from a loss of consciousness (Bewußtsein) during his attacks, they were not epileptic in nature.[111] Rather, Muhammad suffered from *Hysteria Muscularis*[112], a disease accompanied by hallucinations. "The visions of religious enthusiasts," he declared, "are probably mostly, perhaps without exception, a symptom of Hysteria, except that the patients are not preoccupied with physical but with mental excitements; in both-deluded subjects and visionaries – subjective perceptions hold the preponderance over objective impressions."[113] Weil's deluded epileptic is opposed by Sprenger's deceived hysteric. But Sprenger went still further. Utilising the work of the German clinician Johannes Schönlein, Sprenger maintained that hysterics have a tendency to deceit and imposture.[114] The deluded becomes the deceiver. Traditionally, as we have seen, Muhammad was perceived as having invented his revelations to excuse his epilepsy. But in Sprenger, not only delusion but also imposture are the inevitable accompaniments of Muhammad's condition. The myth was medically verified.

Sprenger's account of Muhammad was noticed by the Victorians. In a review of Sprenger's work in *The Edinburgh Review* in 1866, Sprenger's diagnosis of *Hysteria Muscularis* is endorsed, as is also his claim that its victims are both deceived and deceiving: "a tendency to hallucination is the almost invariable concomitant of the hysterical affection. Hallucination is turned by the hysterical patient into an indisputable and cardinal fact; becomes a part of his theory of life and consciousness, and all other considerations and evidences are made to support it. From being self-deceived, the patient proceeds by inappreciable modes of reasoning, to the

---

109 Howden, "The Religious Sentiment", p. 495.
110 See Sprenger, *The Life of Mohammed*, p. 114.
111 See Sprenger, *Das Leben*, i. 208.
112 See *ibid.*, i. 207.
113 *Ibid.*, i. 231; see also Sprenger, *Mohammed*, pp. 8–9, 15.
114 See *ibid.*, i. 210ff.

deception of others."[115] Koelle seized delightedly on Sprenger's theory to reinforce his argument that Muhammad's sincerity was not to be lauded. In his case, not only history but also medical science could be grist to his prejudiced mill: "it has been ascertained by medical observation that such hysterical subjects frequently develop a tendency to dissimulation and deception, and this they seek to conceal so dexterously from themselves and others, that it requires experienced skill to detect it."[116] More unexpectedly, we find it too in Edward Palmer's 1880 introduction to his translation of the Quran for Friedrich Max Müller's *Sacred Books of the East* series. Although not citing Sprenger, he was obviously dependent upon him. According to Palmer, Muhammad's first revelations

> were the almost natural outcome of his mode of life and habit of thought and especially of his physical constitution. From youth upwards he had suffered from a nervous disorder which tradition calls epilepsy, but the symptoms of which more closely resemble certain hysterical phenomena well known and diagnosed in the present time, and which are almost always accompanied with hallucinations, abnormal exercise of the mental functions, and not infrequently with a certain amount of deception, both voluntary and otherwise.[117]

For those who took the most sympathetic view of Muhammad's character, the questions of epilepsy, catalepsy, *Hysteria Muscularis* and so on, were often ignored. Many who were willing to accept Muhammad's sincerity were not willing to do so at the cost of endorsing an image of Muhammad as psychologically aberrant. As the *British Quarterly Review* put it in 1872, "the early Suras of the Koran, though they may be the outpourings of a heated enthusiasm, are certainly not the ravings of a madman. Whatever share in the matter we may choose to attribute to physical causes, the moral position of Mahomet... remains untouched."[118] But in those accounts which did attempt to relate Muhammad's physical and mental constitutions to his inspired states, ambiguity remained. For some, the medical diagnosis of Muhammad as an epileptic established his good faith, but on the understanding that he was deluded. But for others, medical diagnoses, while they suggested he was deceived, intimated he was also deceptive. If for most he was the sincere hero, for many he became the hysterical heretic.[119]

115 *The Edinburgh Review*, 1866, p. 20.
116 Koelle, *Mohammed and Mohammedanism*, p. 56.
117 Palmer, *The Qu'rān*, p. xx.
118 *British Quarterly Review*, 1872, p. 119; see also Grant, *The Religions of the World*, pp. 19–20.
119 Most modern Western Islamicists have abandoned the notion of Muhammad as an epileptic. In part, this is a result of more sophisticated analyses of Muhammad's experien-

7. From Mecca to Medina

The issue of Muhammad's character, of his aims and motivations, was not however simply a matter of imposture or sincerity, of enthusiasm or fraudulent fanaticism. There was also the question of the consistency of his character; more specifically, the issue of the relationship between the Meccan prophet and the Medinan politician. That there had been a change after the hijra, when Muhammad migrated from Mecca to Medina, few among nineteenth century commentators were in doubt. And of course, they were right. From that time, Islam was to develop not only as a religion, but also as a social and political system. But the question was, how substantial was the change, and what did it suggest of him who had inspired it?

The pattern for nineteenth century discussions was set by Edward Gibbon towards the end of the previous century. In his *The History of the Decline and Fall of the Roman Empire*, Gibbon suggested that the Muhammad of the Medinan period was an ambitious politician for whom fraud, perfidy, cruelty, and injustice served to propagate the faith and who secretly smiled at the enthusiasm of his youth and the credulity of his proselytes: "From enthusiasm to imposture," wrote Gibbon, "the step is perilous and slippery: the daemon of Socrates affords a memorable instance, how a wise man may deceive himself, how a good man may deceive others, how the conscience may slumber in a mixed and muddled state between self-illusion and voluntary fraud."[120]

There were a number of aspects of Muhammad's behaviour during the Medinan period which were perceived as evidence of this change. One of these was the use of force. To Charles Mills, in 1818, the Meccan portions of the Quran breathed a spirit of toleration while those of the Medinan period speak nothing but persecution.[121] According to the Anglican divine Henry Hart Milman in his well received *History of Latin Christianity*, Muhammad was a gentle preacher until he unsheathed his sword; but "the sword once unsheathed is the one remorseless argument."[122] The *British Quarterly Review* for 1872 argued that, after the flight from Mecca to Medina, the peaceful preacher became the ruler and the conqueror, the religious sect became a political commonwealth, and the teaching of faith and righteousness became the legislation for a new-born state. Although Muhammad had not abused the trappings of power, "Yet his policy was now of the earth, earthy; in becoming a

ces that date from at least Tor Andrae's *Mohammed* in 1936; in part, as a result of the realization that the historical evidence is too opaque for such speculations.
120 Gibbon, *Decline and Fall*, iii. 162.
121 See Mills, *An History*, p. 368; see also p. 22.
122 Milman, *History*, ii. 23–4; see also anon., *Life of Mohammad*, 1851, p. 57; Green, *The Life of Mahomet*, p. 214; Bush, *The Life of Mohammed*, p. 159.

ruler and a warrior he had become a man of craft and a man of blood."[123] *Harper's New Monthly Magazine* in 1877 too saw the hijra as the end of the pure and peaceful religion of Islam. The hijra, it colourfully declared, turned Muhammad into a political chief, "preaching the efficacy of the temporal sword instead of universal charity, hanging like a blazing flame of destruction over the nations, the omen of bloodshed, desolation, despair."[124]

To Muslims themselves, there is no conflict between Muhammad the prophet and Muhammad the statesman. Indeed, his joint role is the proof of his unique status as the messenger of God.[125] For the Victorians, it was a problem. Imbued with the image of a crucified Messiah, destroyed by the State, the success of Muhammad was an enigma. As Milman put it, "To the question whether Mohammed was hero, sage, impostor, or fanatic, or blended, and blended in what proportions, these conflicting elements in his character? The best reply is the favourite reverential phrase of Islam, 'God knows.'"[126]

But few were willing to remain in such a state of uncertainty. For some, the acquisition of power in Medina entailed that Muhammad no longer had to simulate sincerity, toleration, or moderation. The author of *The Life of Mahomet* in 1799, for example, believed that Mohammed was either of a morose and sullen, or of an hasty and passionate temper, for the Medinan period evidenced rancour and revenge as much as determined resolution. But before this, "his cunning and ready wit no doubt pointed out the necessity of disguising his temper."[127] And *The English Encyclopaedia* in 1802 explained his early passiveness and moderation as a consequence only of his lack of power and the strength of his opposition.[128]

On the other hand, there were many who, like Gibbon, were of the opinion that, although Muhammad had begun with a sincere belief in his mission, he had lapsed into fraud and deception. Jean de Sismondi, for instance, in his *A History of the Fall of the Roman Empire* in 1834 declared that, from the time Muhammad adopted the new character of prophet his life lost its purity, his temper its mildness: "policy entered into his religion, fraud mingled more and more with his conduct; and, at the close of his career, we can hardly explain to ourselves how he could be in good

---

123 *British Quarterly Review*, 1872, p. 128; see also Osborn, *Islam*, pp. 45, 90–1.
124 *Harper's*, 1877, p. 407; see also Grant, *The Religions of the World*, pp. 25–6; Johnstone, *Muhammad and his Power*, pp. 226–7; Buckle, *The Beggar*, p. 57; Goldziher, *Introduction*, pp. 9–10, 26–7.
125 See Schimmel, *Muhammad*, pp. 52–3.
126 Milman, *History*, ii. 13; see also *Colburn's*, 1868, pp. 201–2.
127 Anon., *The Life of Mahomet*, 1799, p. 17; see also Paley, *The Works*, p. 409.
128 *The English Encyclopaedia*, 1802, y. 468; see also Koelle, *Mohammed and Mohammedanism*, pp. 109, 115, 473–4.

faith with himself."¹²⁹ Others were less charitable. Take the author of *The Life of Mohammed* in 1847. He declared that the restraint or concealment of the Prophet's early years could never excuse the unbridled sensuality of his years of political authority: "we can apply no softer term than deliberate wickedness to the shameless craft with which he imposed upon the people, by pretending that what was, in others, a degradation and a sin, was granted to him as a special privilege by God!"¹³⁰ In 1856, Latham Browne simply if bluntly remarked, "it is impossible to believe in his sincerity or his madness. He had then become a politician."¹³¹ And Ernst Renan suggested that the perfume of sanctity appeared only at rare intervals in Muhammad's period of activity: "it seems as if, after having believed in his prophetic mission without any mental reservation, he afterwards lost his spontaneous faith... Man is too weak to bear for long a divine mission, and those only are immaculate whom God soon relieves from the burthen of the apostolate."¹³² Arguments to the effect that Muhammad had moved from sincerity to imposture, from enthusiasm to conscious fraud occurred throughout the latter part of the nineteenth century, although whether his imposture was vicious, or his fraud impious remained matters of dispute.¹³³

But for those convinced of the essential good faith of the Prophet throughout his career, explanations had to be found. Vans Kennedy, for example, denied there had been any change, and he specifically argued against Gibbon's charge that Muhammad was guilty of fraud, perfidy, cruelty, and injustice. In fact, he maintained, there was not a single occasion that "could render injustice or perfidy either advantageous or requisite."¹³⁴ Other explanations were mooted. *The Prospective Review* in 1846 ascribed it to the inevitable temptations that accrued as the result of his altered circumstances – political power necessarily corrupts.¹³⁵ Some followed the psychological explanation hinted at by Gibbon. *The Encyclopaedia Britannica* in 1858 quoted Möhler to this effect: "I maintain, that if one admits the possibility of any man's being able to give out his own individual religious impressions, ideas, and thoughts without suspicion for divine inspirations, I cannot perceive the

---

129 Sismondi, *History*, i. 291; see also i. 297.
130 Anon., *The Life of Mohammed*, 1847, p. 89; see also pp. 87–8; *The Foreign Quarterly Review*, 1840, p. 21.
131 Browne, *Biography*, p. 176.
132 Renan, *Studies*, pp. 180–1.
133 See e. g., Dods, *Mohammed*, pp. 18–23; *Dublin University Magazine*, 1873, pp. 469–71; Palmer, *The Qur'ān*, pp. xlvi–vii.
134 Kennedy, "Remarks," p. 432.
135 *The Prospective Review*, 1846, p. 170.

impossibility of his considering God also to be author of all his other inward impulses."[136]

Essentially the same argument was put by Washington Irving. He noted that, during the Medinan period, Muhammad's revelations appeared so opportunistic that they cast doubt on his sincerity. But Irving offered two plausible excuses: on the one hand, that what Muhammad may have uttered as from his own will may have been reported as from the will of God ; and, on the other hand, that "he may have considered his own impulses as divine inspirations; and that, being an agent ordained to propagate the faith, all impulses and conception towards that end might be part of a continued and divine inspiration."[137] This latter explanation was proferred or implied by William Muir, Barthélemy Saint-Hilaire, Bosworth Smith, and Winwood Reade.[138]

8. Muhammad the Prophet?

There is, of course, an enormous gulf between the recognition of Muhammad's belief in his divine mission, and the declaration that Muhammad's belief was a true one. And the vast majority of those who accepted the sincerity of Muhammad, and there *were* many, remained of the opinion that he was deluded in his belief. Still, now and again, there were some who felt able to view Muhammad, not as an Anti-christ or an imposter, nor as merely sincere, but as a true and worthy emissary of the Divine.

In effect, the question of the truth of Muhammad's mission was one that could only feasibly be asked after the middle of the nineteenth century. For it assumed that he was sincere and this, as we have seen, became the dominant perspective only around this time. It was more than merely a question of whether he was a divine scourge against errant Christians. This had been a common motif in Christian discourse about Islam, and part of an apocalyptic vision of the historical process. It was rather a question that reflected a quite different attitude to the relation between history and the divine, for it implied the possibility of revelation, of religious truth

---

136 *The Encyclopaedia Britannica*, 1858, xv. 301; see also *The Christian Remembrancer*, 1855, pp. 113–4; Freeman, *History and Conquests of the Saracens*, pp. 58–9.
137 Irving, *Life of Mahomet*, p. 237.
138 See Muir, *The Life of Moḥammad*, p. 47; Barthélemy Saint-Hilaire, *Mahomet et le Coran*, pp. xiv–xv; Smith, *Mohammed and Mohammedanism*, p. 120; Reade, *The Martyrdom of Man*, p. 267; see also *British Quarterly Review*, 1872, pp. 126–7; Davies, "Mohammed," p. 327.

and values, quite outside of the Christian scheme of things. That it was asked, and, more importantly, that it was occasionally answered in the affirmative, is one of the clearest indications of a developing consciousness in the West of a religious pluralism, of the recognition of the viability of alternative religious world-views.

An early example of this quite radical shift in consciousness was Edward Freeman in 1856. He felt impelled to admit his conviction that Muhammad's belief in his own mission was well-founded. "Surely," he maintained, "a good and sincere man, full of confidence in his Creator, who works an immense reform both in faith and practice, is truly a direct instrument in the hands of God and may be said to have a direct commission from Him. Why may we not recognize Mahomet, no less than other faithful though imperfect servants of God, serving Him faithfully though imperfectly."[139] The *National Review*, two years later, in its review of Muir, Freeman, and Milman, argued that the same laws which hold good for Isaiah and Ezekiel also hold good for Muhammad, so that "it was quite possible for Mahomet to have been such as they were;"[140] and the *British Quarterly Review* for 1872 declared that the earliest preaching of Muhammad at Mecca "could only have been a movement from God himself."[141] Just how far attitudes had changed since the times of Humphrey Prideaux becomes clear in a sermon by George Adam Smith preached to the Baptist Missionary Society in Bradford in 1908:

> When we see so great a personality, so opportune to the circumstances of his time, and so adequate to many of its needs, that he is not only able to unite within his lifetime the scattered tribes of a peninsula as large as Europe west of the Vistula and to hurl them upon the conquest of half the civilised world, but founds a system which should survive himself for twelve centuries as a living missionary force... – this is a phenomenon, which, as religious men, we are bound to confess as one of the direct acts of God.[142]

In this chapter, I have attempted to show the plurality of images of Muhammad that accrued during the nineteenth century, and the way in which old images were sustained, new images created. But these images were themselves composites of various aspects of the personality of Muhammad and of his teachings. Ambition and profligacy, predestination and paradise, the sword and violence, these were some of the parts which went to create the Victorian Muhammad.

---

139 Freeman, *History and Conquest of the Saracens*, pp. 59–60.
140 *National Review*, 1858, p. 158.
141 *British Quarterly Review*, 1872, p. 118.
142 Smith, *Mohammedanism*, p. 13.

CHAPTER TWO

Portraits of the Prophet

1. Ambition and Lust

> Lust and Ambition, *Mirvan*, are the Springs of all his Actions, whilst, without one Virtue, Dissimulation, like a flatt'ring Painter, Bedecks him with the colouring of them all.[1]
>
> Voltaire: *Mahomet the Impostor*

Voltaire's drama *Le Fanatisme ou Mahomet le Prophète* in 1742 depicted Muhammad as an immoral imposter motivated only by lust, ambition, and sexual jealousy. For Voltaire, the figure of the prophet served in this play to illuminate the tyranny and hypocrisy of the clerical class. Its philosophical intention was to portray religion as nothing but self interested imposture. It succeeded so well in this that it was withdrawn from the Parisian stage after its third performance. By 1751, when the play was next staged, Voltaire had modified his opinions of Muhammad. "I made Mahomet more wicked than he was," he wrote to a friend.[2] At the same time, he gave in his *Essai sur les mœurs* a revised estimate of the Prophet. No longer merely deceiving, Muhammad was also deceived. "Mahomet, violently moved by his own ideas like all enthusiasts first recited these ideas in good faith, confirmed them with visions, deceived himself in the deceiving of others, and finally supported with necessary deceits a doctrine which he believed to be good."[3]

In spite of his later softening of attitude, it was Voltaire's drama that had a significant impact in England. An English version of the play, adapted and translated by James Miller, was performed at the Theatre Royal in Drury Lane in 1743 and 1744, with Garrick himself taking the role of the hero Zaphna. Between 1747 and 1883, there were a further ten editions of the play. As early as 1842, there was criticism of the image of Muhammad portrayed by Voltaire, testimony both to the influence of Voltaire and to changing images of Muhammad. As *The Encyclopaedia Britannica* put it, "Sacrificing truth to scenic effect, and perhaps also to the pleasure of declaiming against what he calls fanaticism, he [Voltaire] has represented his hero

---

1 Miller, *Mahomet the Impostor*, p. 12.
2 Quoted by Bosworth, "Dramatisation," p. 113.
3 Voltaire, *Œuvres Complètes*, xv. 314–5.

as a man of obscure origin, and a monster of cruelty and injustice, in order to present the contrast of extreme baseness with the most undeserved elevation."4

Of course, one can only speculate on the impact that the caricature of Muhammad presented by Voltaire must have had on English audiences over a hundred years of consecutive productions. But even in 1743, when Voltaire's Muhammad became known to the English public, the image of the Prophet as a lustful and ambitious charlatan was not a new one. Voltaire had merely dramatised that which Humphrey Prideaux had succinctly declared forty years earlier: "His two predominant Passions were *Ambition* and *Lust*. The course which he took to gain Empire, abundantly shews the former; and the multitude of Women which he had to do with, proves the later."5

As early as 1720, an almost lone voice was raised in protest. In his "A Defence of Mahomet," Abdulla Mahumed Omar argued that Muhammad's ends were purely religious, and that his political aims were subservient to that. The author, writing against Prideaux in defence of Islam, maintained that only by making himself the political leader was Muhammad able to unite his followers and fix his religion among them, "which Necessity sufficiently clears him from the Imputation of Ambition."6 And a century later, Vans Kennedy inveighed against Christian writers who misled their readers "by gravely informing them that Muhammed acted from a design to satisfy his lust, and to raise himself to the supreme government of his country."7

But in spite of these few caveats, the discourse of lust and ambition remained firmly wedded to that of imposture during the late eighteenth and the first half of the nineteenth centuries, especially in those lives of Muhammad written for a popular audience. In 1796, for example, Thomas Alcock saw Muhammad as merely calling in the aid of religion to make his religious and legislative institutions secure and respectable.8 A sixpenny pamphlet in 1815 simply declared that "ambition, and the desire of satisfying his sensuality were the principle motives of his undertaking."9 And the anonymous *History of Mahomet, The Great Imposter* in 1821 explained Islam as a means invented by Muhammad solely for a political end, namely, the supreme government of his country.10

4 *The Encyclopaedia Britannica*, 1842, xiv. 32.
5 Prideaux, *The True Nature of Imposture*, pp. 137–8; see also p. 12; Addison, *The Life and Death of Mahumed*, p. 35.
6 *Miscellanea Aurea*, p. 170.
7 Kennedy, "Remarks," p. 425.
8 Alcock, *The Rise of Mahomet*, pp. 20–1.
9 Anon., *Life and Actions of Mahomet*, 1815, p. 8.
10 See anon., *The History of Mahomet*, 1821, p. 6; see also *The Edinburgh Encyclopaedia*, 1830, xiii. i. 283.

Prideaux's work remained dominant, especially in the popular Lives. His language was often utilised, if seldom acknowledged. William Sime, for example, echoed Prideaux in 1837 when he wrote "ambition and lust were the passions which reigned supremely in his breast;"[11] and the Reverend George Akehurst in his 1859 pamphlet, the title of which alone indicates its indebtedness to Prideaux, simply paraphrased Prideaux: "His two predominant passions were ambition and lust; the former is manifest in his love of empire, and the latter in the number of women he kept."[12]

Still, after the middle of the century, the language of ambition, like that of imposture, appeared less and less frequently. To be sure, there are instances of it among the more strident of anti-Muslim polemicists until the end of the nineteenth and into the twentieth centuries.[13] But, to all intent and purposes, with the advent of the heroic prophet in the middle of the century, Voltaire's and Prideaux's lustful, ambitious politician went into decline. Indeed, the dominant image of Muhammad became that of a man who acted in a way quite contrary to the successful pursuit of political ambition. As Edith Holland put it in 1914, "There could have been no thought of worldly ambition in his mind, for Mohammed was a rich man, a member of the ruling tribe, and might have risen to a high position in the administration of his native town. He chose, however, to pursue a course which brought on him the enmity of the most powerful of the Meccan chiefs."[14]

2. Muhammad and the Sword

> If one thinks of the Buddha as sitting in a state of contemplation under the Bo-tree, the Prophet can be imagined as a rider sitting on a steed with the sword of justice and discrimination in his hand and galloping at full speed...[15]
>
> S. N. Nasr, *Ideals and Realities of Islam*

The issue of Muhammad's political ambition was intimately linked to that of Muhammad's and later Islam's use of force to propagate the religious, social, and political unity that was Islam. For Muslims themselves, from the earliest times, the

11 Sime, *History of Mohammed*, p. 41.
12 Akehurst, *Imposture Instanced*, p. 20; see also anon., *Life of Mohammad*, 1851, p. 117.
13 See, e.g., Koelle, *Mohammed and Mohammedanism*, pp. 49–50; Menezes, *The Life and Religion of Mahommed*, pp. 151–2.
14 Holland, *The Story of Mohammed*, p. 65.
15 Nasr, *Ideals*, p. 74.

proof of the truth of Muhammad's commission and of his teaching was the success of Islam during the Prophet's life and the expansion of Islamic power in the century after his death.

The extraordinary success of Islam was also, not surprisingly, a topic of considerable importance, both theologically and politically, throughout the medieval and early modern periods and it continued to be so until the middle of the nineteenth century.[16] As with so many other aspects of the interpretation of Islam, the tone in eighteenth and nineteenth century discussions of Islam and violence was set by Prideaux. He warned his readers that it was the universal doctrine of all Muslims that their religion was to be propagated by the sword[17], although he went on to point out that God, in his all-wise Providence allowed Islam to continue as a scourge to Christians "who having receiv'd so holy and so excellent a Religion... will not yet conform ourselves to live worthy of it."[18]

The stress on the use of force in Islam as a means of propagating the faith was, of course, part of an argument concerning the relative truth value of Christianity and Islam. According to this, the success of Islam was due solely to the sword, the success of Christianity, having abjured the sword, was therefore due only to divine favour. Such an argument was implicit in all those who declared that Islam's success was mainly, if not solely, the result of its innate tendency to violence. Isaac Barrow for example, in one of the seventeenth century's most vituperative attacks on Islam declared, "it diffused itself by rage and terrour of arms; convincing mens minds only by the sword, and using no other arguments but blows."[19]

Such traditional images of Islam were still in vogue a century later. Until Muhammad adopted the sword, claimed Bishop Beilby Porteus in 1800, "the number of his proselytes was a mere nothing."[20] Implicit too were traditional European fears of Islam. As one anonymous writer put it in 1847, "The stream of blood which began to flow when Mohammed first unleashed his heaven-directed sword, was to be swelled by the active zeal of the khalifs, till it spread, in a frightful inundation, over the fairest realms of the east and the west."[21] In the same year, Frederick D. Maurice was to go as far as to argue that military conquest was of the essence of Islam: "Mahometanism can only thrive while it is aiming at conquest."[22]

16 See Daniel, *Islam and the West*, pp. 109–33.
17 Prideaux, *The True Nature of Imposture*, p. 33.
18 *Ibid.*, p. 116.
19 Tillotson, *The Works*, ii. 183.
20 Porteus, *A Summary*, p. 72; see also Paley, *The Works*, p. 409.
21 Anon., *The Life of Mohammed*, 1847, p. 104.
22 Maurice, *The Religions of the World*, p. 28; see also Akehurst, *Imposture instanced*, p. 12; Browne, *Biography*, p. 145.

The explicit argument that Islam's success was due to the sword, Christianity's to God, had been popularized in 1734 in George Sale's translation of the Quran. According to him, "It is certainly one of the most convincing proofs that Mahommedism was no other than a human convention, that it owed its progress and establishment to the sword; and it is one of the strongest demonstrations of the divine original of Christianity that it prevailed against all the force and powers of the world by the mere dint of its own truth, after having stood the assaults of all manner of persecutions as well as other oppositions, for three hundred years together..."[23]

Sale's argument continued to be influential well into the nineteenth century. Although the major source for the *Encyclopaedia Britannica's* entry on "Mahomet" in 1797 was Prideaux, the above words of Sale were quoted verbatim, albeit without acknowledgement, and they re-appeared in the same entry in the 1810, 1817, 1823 and 1842 editions.[24] In the 1842 edition, in the entry on "Mohammedanism", a similar argument appeared. The history of the diffusion of Christianity, we read, presents the most striking evidence of its divine origin. But, it went on, "it is not so with Islamism, which, engendered in fanaticism, was propagated by the sword, and established by terror, by conquest, and by extermination."[25] Forty years later, William Muir in a popular essay for *The Leisure Hour* declared that, as an instrument for the propagation of the faith, "the use of the sword is abjured by the Gospel, while it is commanded by the Coran,"[26] although he recognised that in the case of Christianity, practice may often have differed widely from precept.

Muir was not the first to make a distinction between precept and practice in Christianity. As early as 1720, Prideaux was criticised for failing to recognise that Christian practice often differed from Christian precept. Abdulla Mahumed Omar not unreasonably complained, "I suppose he [Prideaux] does not contend, that all Manner of War betwixt Princes is unlawful and against the *Gospel*; if that be his Opinion, let him convince his Christians of it first, who are almost always at War with one another."[27] It is, of course, not merely fortuitous that those most virulent against Islam for its use of force made little either of Christianity's own internecine warfare or of Christianity's agression against Islam. But for those who, accepting the Enlightenment ideal of toleration, decried violence between and by Christians

---

23 Sale, *The Koran*, p. 38; see also Pailin, *Attitudes to Other Religions*, p. 103.
24 *Encyclopaedia Britannica*, 1797, x. 455; *Encyclopaedia Britannica*, 1810, xii. 404; *Encyclopaedia Britannica* 1817, xii. 404; *Encyclopaedia Britannica*, 1823, xii. 404; *The Encyclopaedia Britannica*, 1842, xiv. 28.
25 *The Encyclopaedia Britannica*, 1842, xiv. 40; see also *The North British Review*, 1855, pp. 467–8; Osborn, *Islam*, p. 54; but cf. Blyden, *Christianity*, pp. 248–9.
26 Muir, "Islam and Christianity," p. 134.
27 *Miscellanea Aurea*, p. 185.

against others, much of Christian history was to be condemned. For Isaac Taylor, for example, even in 1834 still very much a deist, *all* religious fanaticism was to be rejected, including that of Christianity: "the Crusades poured a feculent deluge... upon the afflicted Palestine. The dregs, the scum, and the cream of the western world – its nobility and its rabble, in promiscuous rout, flowed towards the sepulchre at the foot of Calvary."[28]

The Western image of a benign Christianity over against a malevolent Islam was a mythical one; for, with few exceptions, it ignored both the violence often attendant on the extension of the Christian faith, and the religious tolerance which often accompanied the spread of Islam. But the myth did reflect a deep-seated Western fear, always potent in the imagination, and sometimes grounded in reality – the fear of the West being overwhelmed by the East. During the nineteenth century, however, such a fear began to fade.

In his *Islam, Europe and Empire*, Norman Daniel argues that, while the image of Islam as a religion essentially of force remained throughout the early part of the nineteenth century, it came to be seen more in relation to entirely new political realities. In essence, the cultural and political power of the West rendered effete the traditional Western fear of being engulfed by Asia in general, by Islam in particular. As Daniel puts it, "Islam, the religion of force, was beginning to be dominated by the greater force of Europe; the old enemy was becoming a subject, or, if not a subject, he was being compelled to accept Western influences as a result of Western prosperity."[29]

In the Victorian period, the cultural power of the West over the East allowed for the possibility of some modifications to the traditional image of Islam as a religion of force and violence. On the one hand, it could be argued that, while an aggressive Islam needed to be opposed, a peaceful Islam was impotent, and only fit for cultural improvement. A clear example of this style of argument is provided by Marcus Dods in his *Mohammed, Buddha, and Christ*. Fruitful in aggression, Islam is sterile when quiescent:

> It has been a religion of opposition from the first, living by aggression, mighty and purifying while it flows in full flood, but when resting and at peace, it stagnates and throws up a filthy and putrid scum... when the victory is won, and men have to shape a life of peace for themselves, there is nothing in this creed to guide or to sustain.[30]

On the other hand, the use of force in Islam could be justified or at least down-

---

28 Taylor, *Fanaticism*, p. 174.
29 Daniel, *Islam, Europe and Empire*, p. 240.
30 Dods, *Mohammed*, pp. 11–12.

played. Johann Moehler in 1847, for example, recognised that Muhammad had endorsed the use of the sword but nevertheless he wished to justify the Prophet's actions on the grounds that Muhammad did not know the difference between nationalism and religion. For his followers, he suggested, the prophet and the politician were indistinguishable.[31] This, in part, was a plea not to judge Islam on latter day Protestant understandings of the separation of Church and State. Isaac Taylor similarly excused the actions of Muhammad: "Mohammed perhaps had convinced himself that so worthy and holy a purpose [as a divine reformation of the world] would well excuse any means that might bring it about. Christian doctors have entertained the same principle, and have made a worse use of it..."[32] To R. Bosworth Smith, the sword was to become an essential part of Islam, as a consequence of which it was immeasurably below Christianity. Nevertheless, he argued, the exigencies of Muhammad's situation in Medina merited his use of the sword[33]; and, after all, Christianity itself was not averse to using *violence* to spread the faith.[34]

Some remained unconvinced by Smith's apology. *The Quarterly Review* in 1877, in its review of Smith's work, maintained that Islam's reliance on the power of the sword detracted from its character as a divine institution.[35] But despite this, the Islamic use of force is no longer perceived as a threat to the Empire or its possessions: "... the fact that the name of our most gracious Sovereign is now inserted in the Khutbeh, or 'Friday bidding prayer,' in all mosques throughout India, is a sufficient proof that Islam is not antagonistic either to religious or political toleration, and that the doctrine of Jehád, or holy war, is not so dangerous or barbarous an one as is generally imagined."[36]

Just how little of a political threat Islam had become in the early part of the twentieth century is clear from Edith Holland's *The Story of Mohammed*, written for the adolescent reader in a series entitled *Heroes of all Time*. Like Smith, she suggested that it was the circumstances of Muhammad's life in Medina that justified the use of force.[37] But, writing in the context of England's conflict with Germany in 1914, she held up Muhammed and his followers as examples to be followed. "Although we believe," she wrote, "that religion should teach us peace, and not war, yet we cannot but admire the zeal of these early Moslems, who were ready to

---

31 See Moehler, *On the Relation of Islam*, p. 27.
32 Taylor, *Fanaticism*, p. 160; see also *Colburn's*, 1868, pp. 194–5.
33 See Smith, *Mohammed and Mohammedanism*, pp. 168–71.
34 See *ibid.*, pp. 184–5.
35 *The Quarterly Review*, 1877, p. 230; see also Badger, "Mohammed," p. 96; but cf. East, *The Last Days of Great Men*, p. 295.
36 *Ibid.*, p. 231.
37 Holland, *The Story of Mohammed*, p. 109.

give their lives, their property and all they had, in the cause of their faith." Just as, one might add, Holland's readers might be expected to give their all in the cause of their country.[38]

For a number of writers sympathetic to Islam, the argument that Islam's success was due to the sword was greatly exaggerated. As early as the 1670's, Henry Stubbe decried it as a vulgar opinion that Muhammad propagated his doctrine by the sword. Although he recognised that Muslims engaged in war, this was not for the propagation of their religion, but rather for the enlargement of their Empire: "so that when we say that the Religion of Mahomet was propagated by the Sword, we must understand it only as a consequence of their Victories, and not that they forced Men by Slaughters and Murders into their Opinion."[39] And the anonymous author of *Historical and Critical Reflections upon Mahometanism and Socinianism* in 1712, while he was willing to admit that violence had some place in the propagation of Islam, suggested that persuasion had more.[40]

Certainly, in the nineteenth century, as for Stubbe, the use of force was often seen, not so much as one of the causes of the success of Islam, but as one of its effects. In his apology for Islam in 1829, Godfrey Higgins argued precisely this. "The sword," he said, "is of no value without a hand to use it; and it was the enthusiasm of the persons who used it which gave them the victory."[41] But it was Carlyle who refined this argument and secured its popularity:

> The sword indeed: but where will you get your sword! Every new opinion, at its starting, is precisely in a *minority of one*. In one man's head alone, there it dwells as yet. One man alone of the whole world believes it; there is one man against all men. That *he* take a sword, and try to propagate with that, will do little for him. You must first get your sword: I will allow a thing to struggle for itself in this world, with any sword or tongue or implement it has, or can lay hold of. We will let it preach and pamphleteer, and fight, and to the uttermost bestir itself, and do, beak and claws, whatsoever is in it; very sure that it will, in the long run, conquer nothing which does not deserve to be conquered.[42]

---

38 *Ibid.*, p. 111.
39 Stubbe, *An Account*, p. 188.
40 See anon., *Historical and Critical Reflections*, p. 170.
41 Higgins, *An Apology*, p. 70; see also *The Foreign Quarterly Review*, 1833, p. 203.
42 Carlyle, *On Heroes*, p. 61.

And Carlyle's opinion was much cited, usually supported throughout the Victorian period.[43]

Although, as we have seen, the traditional image of Islam as having succeeded through its use of force held sway throughout the nineteenth century, it was balanced by a number of motifs. Images of Islam's use of persuasion rather than force co-alesced with those of Carlyle's charismatic leader; Muhammad's justified use of violence was counterpointed by Christianity's unjustified use of it. Such images were themselves facilitated by a burgeoning imperial confidence in which Islamic culture was seen, not so much as a political threat, but rather as a sphere of Western patronage, both religious and secular.

3. Predestination and Fatalism

> Naught shall visit us but what God has prescribed for us; He is our Protector; in God let the believers put all their trust.
>
> Quran 9.51

> Yet I am All-forgiving to him who repents and believes, and does righteousness, and at last is guided.
>
> Quran 20.84

The doctrine of predestination or its more secular counterpart fatalism was also seen as a factor in the military success of Islam. As Henry Stubbe put it in the 1670's, "It is certain that in reference to the Soldiery none venture their Lives in Battle, like those who suppose they cannot dye before their appointed time, that all the Contrivances of Men depend upon the Sovereign Will of God, that there is no such thing as chance, nor any mistakes in the management of human Affairs but all are swayed by Destiny."[44] For Stubbe himself, there was nothing improper in this. He saw predestination, as a tenet of Judaism and early Christianity, proved by arguments in both the Old and New Testaments. Indeed, he exclaimed, "O. Cromwell made this observation in the late Civil Warr, and gave no encouragement to such Preachers as taught the contrary."[45]

Both Islam and Christianity were committed to what, on the face of it were

---

43 See e.g., *The Christian Remembrancer*, 1855, p. 141; *The Encyclopaedia Britannica*, 1853–60, xv. 302; *Dublin University Magazine*, 1876, pp. 143–4; Grant, *The Religions of the World*, pp. 34–5.
44 Stubbe, *An Account*, p. 179.
45 *Ibid.*, p. 179.

incompatible intellectual demands: Religiously, both were committed to the doctrine of God's omnipotence with its implied divine determinism; and ethically, both were committed to the moral responsibility of the individual for his conduct. And both traditions have a long history of attempts to resolve this dilemma. Thus, although Stubbe and others tended to ignore the role of freewill in Islamic theology, his uncritical account of Islamic predestination was not untypical. Christians in the pre-Reformation period, themselves committed to predestination (however qualified) did not criticise the Islamic doctrine. And Post-reformation Protestants could hardly cavil at a theory so central to their own positions, although some concern was expressed about the propriety of the heavenly rewards Muslims gained from military martyrdom. As the anonymous author of a 1712 life of Muhammad put it, "'Tis certain, nothing could more encourage his Men to fight valiantly, than the Belief of a Doctrine which teaches, that whatever Dangers they should expose themselves to, yet they could not die sooner or later than was unalterably predetermin'd they should; and that... they should obtain the Happiness of becoming Martyrs, and thereby merit a Place in Paradise, where they should have the full and undisturb'd Enjoyment of beautiful young Women, pleasant Gardens, fine Rivers and delicious Wines."[46]

If the Muslim doctrine of predestination was, to some extent, immune from criticism by virtue of Christian analogies to it, its psychological correlate in the individual was not. During the seventeenth, eighteenth and nineteenth centuries, fatalism was to establish itself among Western writers as an indelible mark of Islamic societies, in contrast to Western ones. As early as 1678, for example, Thomas Smith, in his work on the religion, manners, and government of the Turks, declared, they "still retain the absurd principle of fate, which is the genuine issue of their gross ignorance and barbarousness."[47] Such judgements were to become more common in an imperialist context. In 1826, T. Perronet Thompson, member of Parliament, Fellow of the Royal Society, and utilitarian philosopher, although not unsympathetic to Islam, saw Islamic fatalism as having contributed to the ultimate inferiority of Muslims in policy and war. Belief in predestination had once been seen as a cause of Islamic military success; its psychological effect – fatalism – was now seen, in a context where Europe was dominant, as a source of failure: "The distinction between the Oriental and the European genius lies in the [latter's] *téte organisante*, or the habit of laying long-drawn trains for the compassing of an uncertain end."[48]

46 Anon., "The Life and Actions of Mahomet, extracted chiefly from Mahometan Authors," in *Four Treatises*, pp. 64–5; see also e.g., Paley, *The Works*, p. 408; Sismondi, *History*, i. 294–5.
47 Smith, *Remarks*, p. 108; see also Blunt, *A Voyage*, p. 155.
48 Thompson, "Arabs and Persians," p. 224; see also *The Christian Remembrancer*, 1855, p. 146.

Intellect and will would always defeat, according to Thompson, the fatalism of indifference.

Predestination and fatalism were also linked to the image of Islamic governments as despotic. *The Foreign Quarterly Review* in 1833, for instance, suggested that men's notions of God were always modified by their notions of civil government. The extravagant fatalism of the Quran is one of the greatest recommendations of it for, it argued, "the notion of absolute predestination and irrespective decrees is natural to the mind of one who is ruled by a despot."[49] William Palgrave refined the image further. Allah, the God of Islam was an arbitrary Oriental despot. God, he exclaimed, "burns one individual through all eternity amid red-hot chains and seas of molten fire, and seats another in the plenary enjoyment of an everlasting brothel between forty celestial concubines, just and equally for his own good pleasure, and because he wills it."[50] The despotism of the few and the apathy of the many were, for Robert Osborn, the result of what he saw as Islam's central tenet – fatalism; and it was this that explained the degraded condition of Islamic countries, their utter exhaustion and swift corruption.[51]

For those least sympathetic to Islam, the image of resigned, indolent, fatalistic Muslims was an important part of anti-Islamic argument. In general, nineteenth century writers who were sympathetic to Islam, while not denying the fatalism inherent in Islamic cultures, nevertheless attempted to separate it from Muhammad and the origins of Islam. This was effected in a number of ways. Charles Mills for example, argued that, although Muhammed preached predestination in the strongest terms, the Prophet never denied the necessity of religious and moral endeavour.[52] Somewhat similarly, *The Eclectic Magazine* in 1862, in its review of Muir's *The Life of Mohammed*, suggested that the fatalism "now universal in the Mohammedan world, was no idea of the Prophet;"[53] while *The Quarterly Review* in 1869 observed that, as far as Muhammad and the Quran were concerned, fatalism was an utter and absolute invention: "nothing was further from his mind than that pious state of idle and hopeless inanity and stagnation."[54]

Another popular defense was the comparison of the Islamic doctrine of predestination with that of Christianity. R. Bosworth Smith, for instance, emphasised the variety of schools in Islam which differed on the relationship between predestination and free will. He maintained too that Muhammad himself would have had

49 *The Foreign Quarterly Review*, 1833, p. 202.
50 Palgrave, *Narrative*, i. 368.
51 See Osborn, *Islam*, pp. 26–7; see also, *The National Quarterly Review*, 1876, p. 222; Grant, *The Religions of the World*, pp. 41–2.
52 See Mills, *An History*, pp. 293–4.
53 *The Eclectic Magazine*, 1862, p. 35. The author was Meredith Townsend.
54 *The Quarterly Review*, 1869, p. 349; see also Lane-Poole, *Studies*, pp. 90–1.

more in common with Pelagius than Augustine, and with Arminius than Calvin.[55] This was undoubtedly a useful piece of apologetic in a mid-Victorian religious context which itself, at least in practice, was more committed to the individual's ultimate moral and religious responsibility for himself than to a passive reliance on divine predestination. *Chamber's Encyclopaedia* in 1874 went still further. It argued that the Islamic system, taken as a whole, sufficed to prove that Augustinian predestination was not taught in the Quran.[56] While for Smith and *Chamber's*, the defence of Muhammad entailed mimimising the role of predestination in Islam, for Marcus Dods, true to his Presbyterian heritage, it meant defending Muhammad as a *true* predestinationist. He argued that the fatalism of the East was a matter of race rather than religion, and he contrasted the apathy of the Turks with the Arabian sense of moral responsibility. Muhammad, he declared, was certainly as thorough a predestinarian as Calvin, but just as little of a fatalist.[57]

4. Pleasures and Paradise

> Old Mahometanism is lingering about, just ready to drop... Think of the poor dear houris in Paradise, how sad they must look as the arrivals of the Faithful become less and less frequent every day... I can fancy... the fountains of eternal wine are beginning to run rather dry... the ready-roasted-meat trees may cry, "Come eat me," every now and then in a faint voice without any gravy in it – but the Faithful begin to doubt the quality of the victuals. Of nights you may see the houris sitting sadly under them, darning their faded muslins: Ali, Omar and the Imaums are reconciled and have gloomy consultations; and the Chief of the Faithful himself... sits alone in a tumbledown kiosk, thinking moodily of the destiny that is impending over him; and of the day when his gardens of bliss shall be as vacant as the bankrupt Olympus.
>
> William Thackeray: *Journey from Cornhill to Grand Cairo*

It was the political decline of Turkey that motivated William Thackeray in 1844 to sketch an Islamic Paradise with a progressively decreasing population. In so doing, Thackeray was bearing witness, albeit inversely, to the very traditional attribution of the success of Islamic arms to the sensual paradise offered as a reward to its fallen warriors. From a very early period, Islam was viewed as a religion of violence and

---

55 See Smith, *Mohammed and Mohammedanism*, pp. 164–5; see also *The Quarterly Review*, 1877, pp. 229–30.
56 See *Chamber's Encyclopaedia*, 1874, vi. 509.
57 See Dods, *Mohammed*, pp. 52–3.

sensuality.[58] And the Muslim view of Paradise typified for both Western and Eastern Christendom their vision of Islam as a non-spiritual, sensual religion.[59]

It was an image that was to survive until the end of the nineteenth century. As late as 1882, for example, T. C. Trowbridge, in a savage critique of the Turks, explained their decadence as the result of Islam's notion of Paradise: "The masses of the Christians," he wrote, "are virtuous; the masses of the Turks are thoroughly depraved; they are born, they live and die in an atmosphere of vice. Now it may fairly be asked whether this state of immorality can be traced either directly or indirectly, to the religion of Mohammed. We have not far to go for an answer. The Koran itself sets before those who receive it the joys of a sensual paradise."[60]

The overall image of Paradise in the Quran is of an eternal life that satisfies all human needs and involves human relationships, a life which is sometimes decribed in terms of "wide-eyed houris,"[61] at others in terms of family relationships.[62] But, in the West, the image of a Paradise intended to satisfy male sensuality predominated.

It was often as the direct outcome of Muhammad's own sensuality. A lurid picture of Paradise served to reinforce images of the carnality of the Prophet. According to Thomas Herbert in 1665, "Paradise is a place of as much delight as *Mahomets* carnal apprehension was able to imagine, or his fancy contrive."[63] An anonymous *Life of Mahomet* in 1799 saw Muhammad's view of Paradise as a "tid bit for the stomach of an Arabian, constitutionally addicted to the love of pleasure, and entirely suited to the palate of its voluptuous author."[64] Sismondi in 1834 saw the Paradise of Muhammad as the result of his indulgence in the burning passion of the Arabian temperament which he shared with his countrymen[65]; and William Sime, very much the traditional polemicist, found that the impious representations of the Islamic Paradise "afford additional proofs of the character of its author, who, even on the awful subject of eternal life, could thus revel in sensuality and lust."[66]

A brave attempt was made by William Muir to defend Muhammad from this charge on text-critical grounds. "It is remarkable," he exclaimed, "that the notices in the Ḳorān of this voluptuous Paradise are *almost entireley confined* to a time when, whatever the tendency of his desires, Moḥammed was living a chaste and

---

58 See e.g., Turtledove, *The Chronicle*, p. 35.
59 On medieval images, see Daniel, *Islam and the West*, pp. 148–52.
60 Trowbridge, "Mohammedanism," pp. 284–5.
61 See e.g., *Quran*, 44.54, 52.20, 55.72, 56.22.
62 See e.g., *Quran*, 13.23, 40.8.
63 Herbert, *Some Years Travels*, p. 346.
64 Anon., *The Life of Mahomet*, 1799, p. 28.
65 Sismondi, *History*, i.294.
66 Sime, *History of Mohammed*, p. 48; see also *The Eclectic Magazine*, 1850, p. 53.

temperate life with a wife threescore years of age."⁶⁷ Muir was right. Most of the Quranic references to the sensual pleasures of Paradise may be ascribed to the Meccan period. Still, for those determined to see Muhammad as a voluptuary, the text-critical evidence could be made to support such a view. If sensuality was not a part of Muhammad's life during the Meccan period, the Quranic passages could be re-interpreted as the overt expressions of an unconscious repressed sensuality. The *British Quarterly Review* in 1872, for instance, noted that the detailed passages on Paradise came from the husband of Khadija, and only cursory mentions from the owner of a wellstocked harem in Medina. Such passages, it concluded, even if taken symbolically "could have sprung only from an imagination which dwelt all the more on pleasures from which a virtuous effort of continence had forbidden."⁶⁸

For many commentators, Muhammad's view of Paradise was not so much an accidental product of his own sensuality as the deliberate result of his guile. Many drew, if only incipiently, on the argument that religion was the result of a kingly or priestly conspiracy to bring the mass of the people to submission by imposing false beliefs upon them.⁶⁹ Muhammad's view of Paradise could thus be combined with the image of his worldly ambition. Henry Blunt, for instance, suggested that "*Mahomet* knowing he had not to deal with a *Scholastique* and *Speculative* generation but with a people *rude*, and *sensual* made not his Paradise to consist in *Visions*, and *Hallelujahs*, but in delicious *fare, pleasant Gardens*, and *Wenches* with great eyes..."⁷⁰ According to Humphrey Prideaux, Muhammad's promise of Paradise was cunningly framed to suit the Arabian penchant for sensual pleasure.⁷¹ A century later, in 1796, the same argument was put by Nathan Alcock. Muhammad's Paradise, he declared, "was a well-contrived scheme to allure and captivate the voluptuous inhabitants of the eastern nations... whose warm passions and quick feelings gave them so great a propensity to every species of luxury."⁷²

This correlation of sensuality with the Eastern mind gained a firm foothold in the Western imagination from the beginning of the eighteenth century. This was, in particular, I think, the result of the enormous popularity of Antoine Galland's *Les Mille et Une Nuits* during the eighteenth and nineteenth centuries.⁷³ Galland had stressed the magical and fantastic elements of the *Arabian Nights*, and evoked an image of an exotic and romantic Islam. By the end of the eighteenth century the *Arabian Nights* was a children's classic. As Kathryn Tidrick notes, "Children happy

67 Muir, *The Life of Mohammed*, p. 76.
68 *British Quarterly Review*, 1872, p. 130.
69 See Manuel, *The Changing of the Gods*, pp. 66–8.
70 Blunt, *A Voyage*, pp. 122–3.
71 See Prideaux, *The True Nature of Imposture*, p. 25.
72 Alcock, *The Rise of Mahomet*, p. 32.
73 See especially, Ali, *Scheherazade in England*.

and unhappy grew up with the tales as part of the furniture of their imagination. As adults the word "Arabia" possessed for some of them a special resonance which defied any merely geographical definition."[74] Certainly, the *Arabian Nights* did much to soften negative images of the Muslim East and of Islam.

But it could also provide evidence of the essential voluptuousness of Muhammad and the Arabian mind. It could produce Tennyson's *Recollections of the Arabian Nights*, imbue Goethe with its exoticism, and influence Carlyle's portrait of the Prophet. But it would also beget that classic of the eighteenth century pornographic genre, *The Lustful Turk* in 1828.[75] While the Reverend Samuel Green could appreciate the beauty and moral instruction of the *Arabian Nights*[76], he could also criticise Muhammad for setting forth his promises of Paradise "in colours best calculated to work upon the fancies of a sensitive and sensual race, whose minds, in consequence of their national habits, were little susceptible of the images of abstract enjoyment."[77] And de Lacy Johnstone's *Muhammad and His Power* in 1901 was permeated by the image of the sensual and voluptuous Arabs: "The delights of Muhammad's Paradise are just such sensual joys as appealed most strongly to the Arab mind, – peace and rest under shady trees, with ever-flowing crystal streams, abundance of all manner of dainty food and costly dress, wine that should cheer the heart but not cloud the brain, and, above all dark-eyed virgin brides..."[78] As such, the sensual Paradise of Muhammad was also compared unfavourably with the spiritual, certainly non-sexual, Paradise of the Christian tradition. The contrast of a spiritual Christianity with a material Islam was drawn by Henry Hart Milman in the 1850's. He compared the Islamic image of a heaven and a hell "as a motive to the heart of a ruder, grosser race, with the Christian's calm, vague, trembling anticipations of a beatitude, of which that which was most definite was exemption from the sorrows and sins of life, the companionship of saints and martyrs, or even of the Redeemer himself..."[79]

Those sympathetic to Islam clearly perceived the necessity of neutralising an image of Paradise in Islam so at variance not only with the Christian idea of heaven but also with the traditional canons of Christian morality. A variety of explanations were proposed. One was to the effect that Muhammad portrayed Paradise in

---

74 Tidrick, *Heart-beguiling Araby*, p. 36.
75 See Marcus, *The Other Victorians*, pp. 200–19.
76 See Green, *The Life of Mahomet*, p. 298.
77 *Ibid.*, p. 82; see also Pfander, *Remarks*, pp. 39–40; Mills, *An History*, p. 14.
78 Johnstone, *Muhammad and His Power*, p. 154; see also *The National Quarterly Review*, 1876, pp. 219–20.
79 Milman, *History*, ii. 38–9; see also Dods, *Mohammed*, pp. 49–50. But there were, in the nineteenth century, more "earthy" images of the Christian heaven. See Lang, "The Sexual Life of the Saints."

sensual terms solely as a means to a higher end. As Adrian Reland put it in 1712 in his *Of the Mahometan Religion*, Muhammad "was willing to allow the Body its own Pleasure, that in proposing this Reward he might allure his rude *Arabians* who thought of nothing but what was gross and sensible to fall in with the Worship of one God and his Doctrines."[80] Moreover, he went on to point out, many contended that the words of Muhammad were to be understood parabolically of spiritual pleasures.[81]

That the images of Paradise were to be understood allegorically or metaphorically was perhaps the most common defence. Henry Stubbe, for example, argued that, because Muhammad had copied his ideas on heaven and hell from the Jews and Christians it was unjust to criticise only *his* images of them. And he censured those who interpreted Christian imagery as spiritual Truth but would not allow the same interpretation of analogous Islamic descriptions of Paradise. "For my part," he declared, "I cannot distinguish betwixt the paradise of the Jews and Christians, and that which Mahomet promiseth to his followers, and do think that our Notions of the Torments of the Wicked in a lake of fire and brimstone somewhere underground, hath as much of folly and absurdity in it as in any fable of Mahometans."[82]

Stubbe, like many others, was aware that there was in Islam, as in Christianity, a tradition of an allegorical interpretation of parts of the Quran, alongside more literal interpretations of it.[83] This awareness that there were different modes of interpreting the Quran within Islam continued into the eighteenth and nineteenth centuries, generally with the assumption that the literal interpretation was the earlier, the allegorical later. Thus, in the life of Muhammad added to the 1757 edition of Simon Ockley's *The History of the Saracens*, we read, "These delights of paradise were certainly, at first, understood literally; however Mohammedan divines may have since allegorised them into a spiritual sense."[84] A similar position was taken by Gibbon. He saw Muhammad as having intended to be understood literally although "his modest apologists are driven to the poor excuse of figures and allegories."[85] Even Carlyle saw Muhammad as having thought in literal terms of

---

80 Reland, *Of the Mahometan Religion*, in *Four Treatises*, p. 75; see also Kennedy, "Remarks," p. 438.
81 *Ibid.*, p. 75.
82 Stubbe, *An Account*, p. 167; see also Thompson, "Arabs and Persians," 1735, pp. 216–9; anon., *Reflections on Mohammedism*, 1735, pp. 43–4.
83 See, e.g., Daniel, *Islam and the West*, p. 61.
84 Ockley, *The History of the Saracens*, p. 69. The Life may have been written by Dr. Long, then Master of Pembroke College, Cambridge. See Holt, "Treatment of Arab History," in Lewis and Holt (eds.) *Historians*, p. 295.
85 Gibbon, *Decline and Fall*, iii. 144.

heaven and hell, though he was not averse to giving his own allegorical interpretation: "what is all this but a rude shadow, in the rude Bedouin imagination, of that grand spiritual Fact, and Beginning of Facts, which it is ill for us too if we do not all know and feel: the Infinite Nature of Duty."[86] This was allegorising indeed!

However that may be, nineteenth century apologists for Islam were clearly in something of a dilemma. Fully aware of the presence of literal interpretations of Paradise in Islam, and believing (probably rightly) that Muhammad was thinking in literal terms, they were unable firmly to support the allegorical understanding, thus avoiding the image of a sensual Paradise. On the other hand, unlike Stubbe in the seventeenth century, they couldn't defend literal understandings of Paradise in Islam by comparison with identical Christian understandings. For, during the course of the nineteenth century, the doctrine of hell had been relegated, as Gladstone put it, "to the far corners of the Christian mind... there to sleep in deep shadow as a thing needless in our enlightened and progressive age;"[87] and if the idea of a heavenly life nevertheless continued to play a role, it was in terms much more vague than traditional Biblical imagery had suggested. Faced with this quandary, most Victorian defenders of Islam were more reticent about the issue of Paradise than about other matters.

5. Muhammad and the Miraculous

According to Islamic tradition, Muhammad refused to work miracles to evidence the truth of this message, excepting the Quran. For Christian critics of Islam, his inability so to do was traditionally seen as indicative of the fraudulent character of his assumption of prophethood. Moreover, the necessity to propagate Islam by the use of the sword was ofttimes perceived as the result of his incapacity to work wonders. As William Biddulph exclaimed in 1609, "See the subtiltie of this dissembler and deceiver *Mahomet,* who knowing that he was destitute altogether of the heavenly gift to worke miracles; hee fained that he was sent with the sword."[88] Even as late as 1878, Marcus Dods imputed this to Muhammad: "Other prophets had come with miracles, and had been disbelieved, there Mohammed came with the sword."[89]

86 Carlyle, *On Heroes,* p. 75.
87 Quoted by Rowell, *Hell and the Victorians,* p. 212.
88 Biddulph, *The Travels,* p. 51; see also Blunt, *A Voyage,* pp. 140–1.
89 Dods, *Mohammed,* p. 28.

For Christian apologists, and for anti-Muslim polemicists, the occurrence of the miracles of Christ was clear evidence of the divine foundation of Christianity, and the lack of them in Islam just as clear evidence of its falsity. As Norman Daniel puts it, miracles "were the authentic mark of Christendom, and there was Qur'anic evidence for saying so. That is why the Qur'anic admission that the Prophet could not work miracles was greeted with delight; why the denial of the necessity for them, and the idea that the Qur'ān itself was the miracle, were both ignored or derided."[90]

Such attitudes were to remain common until the middle of the nineteenth century. John Locke, Samuel Clarke, and Joseph Butler all dismissed Muslim claims on the grounds that no confirmatory miracles were offered.[91] Pierre Bayle wondered why Muhammad, perceiving his own inability to perform miracles, persisted in his delusions of prophethood.[92] Enlightenment critiques of miracles and the possibility of miraculous occurrences seemed to have had little impact on such seventeenth and eighteenth century thinkers. In 1785, for example, Joseph White explicitly rejected David Hume's arguments against miracles.[93] And he declared that, just as the miracles of Jesus were evidence of his divine mission and character, Muhammad's unwillingness to do likewise was indicative of his imposture.[94] In 1800, Bishop Beilby Porteus described Muhammad's excuses as "laboured and awkward," in comparison to Jesus, "who worked a great number of the most astonishing miracles in the open face of day..."[95]

Of course, numerous miracles were ascribed to Muhammad in later Islamic biographical traditions. And many eighteenth century commentators were aware of these. But generally, recognising them as being of a late provenance, they dismissed them. William Paley for example, argued that only when Islam was established by conquest did the stories of Muhammad's miracles appear, and that such stories were not part of the Prophet's "authentic history." Consequently, Muhammad's pretensions cannot be verified. In contrast, "Admit to be true almost any part of Christ's history... and he must have come fom God."[96] As David Pailin comments, "Christian apologists ensure that the criteria for authentic miracles can only be satisfactorily met by those miracles which verify their own beliefs."[97]

90 Daniel, *Islam and the West*, p. 77.
91 See Pailin, *Attitudes to Other Religions*, p. 86.
92 See Bayle, *Historical and Critical Dictionary*, ii. 251.
93 See Wollheim (ed.), *Hume on Religion*, pp. 205–29.
94 See White, *Sermons*, pp. 147, 157, 171.
95 Porteus, *A Summary*, pp. 70–1.
96 Paley, *The Works*, p. 406; see also Pfander, *Remarks*, p. 17; for Paley on Hume and miracles, see Le Mahieu, *The Mind of William Paley*.
97 Pailin, *Attitudes to Other Religions*, p. 88.

To be sure, here and there, there were defenses of Islam from this kind of attack. Stubbe, for example, pointed to a Muslim argument that the concurrent testimony of so many miracles was evidence of the truth of Muhammad's apostleship "which plea the Christians themselves make use of, and therefore is not to be lightly rejected."[98] And he defended Muhammad's rejection of the authority of miracles: "There were so many obtruded on the World (especially by the Christians), that he scorned the pretence, and he had these further considerations that true Miracles cannot be distinguished from false by any human Test; that the wicked may do real Miracles; that some Miracles might be derived from Magick or be the effect of some celestial Constellation ruling the nativity of perticular [sic] persons..."[99] Similarly, Boulainvilliers defended Muhammad as an enlightened reasonable man. Neither the Arabians nor the Christians had a right, he argued, to require miracles from a man "who constantly declared and protested that he had no other power than to persuade those who would calmly listen unto him, or to conquer those by force of arms who resisted the force of his *reasons*..."[100]

However that may be, the argument against Islam from miracles continued into the nineteenth century. Thus, for example, William van Mildert, Bishop of Landaff, in his work on *Infidelity*, found it remarkable that Muhammad afforded the first instance "in which the Arch-Deceiver of Mankind [i. e. Satan] attempted to propagate his delusions, without the semblance, at least, of *Miracles*,"[101] an argument which implied that, even if Muhammad had worked miracles, they would have been ascribed by van Mildert to what he elsewhere called "the Author and Worker of all Spiritual Evil,"[102] and not to God. *The Encyclopaedia Britannica* for 1842 took a more reasonable, if historically inaccurate, approach. It suggested that, if Muhammad had not invented the miracles related of him, he nevertheless permitted his followers to do so, and to take advantage of the credulity of the people.[103] And, in spite of its quite sympathetic interpretation of the Prophet, *The Encyclopaedia Britannica* for 1858 simply observed "that the proper proofs of a Divine revelation are miracles and prophecy, and that Islamism possesses neither the one nor the other."[104]

But, remarkably, from this time on, the argument against Islam from miracles disappeared. It is difficult to be clear why a criticism, so common from the medieval

---

98 Stubbe, *An Account*, p. 162.
99 *Ibid.*, p. 160.
100 Boulainvilliers, *The Life of Mahomet*, pp. 249–50.
101 Van Mildert, *Infidelity*, i. 219. It went through four editions between 1806–30.
102 *Ibid.*, i. 227.
103 See *The Encyclopaedia Britannica*, 1842, xiv. 31.
104 *The Encyclopaedia Britannica*, 1853–60, xv. 302.

period to the middle of the nineteenth century, should suddenly vanish from the literature. But we can gather some clues as to the reasons.

In part at least, it was the result of a loss of faith in supernaturalism in general in the mid and late Victorian period, at least among the educated classes. With the growing dominance of the scientific world view, the argument from miracles to the truth of Christianity had lost its intellectual cogency, and the supposed eye-witness evidence to the miraculous its credibility. As Owen Chadwick remarks, "Science could not disprove a single miracle said to have happened, still less could science prove *miracles do not happen*. But the successes of science made ever more powerful the old agnosticism of Hume and the Enlightenment, that on the face of it witnesses are probably wrong."[105] Thus, the argument against Islam from miracles no longer could have anything like the same self-evidentness. Indeed, apologists like Bosworth Smith were now enabled to make, for the first time, a positive virtue out of Islam's lack of the miraculous. Now, it was science that vindicated Muhammad:

> in proportion as exact knowledge advances, the sphere of the supernatural is narrowed; and therefore a proof which is fitted for an imaginative and creative age is not best suited for a critical and scientific one. Many minds, no doubt, will always crave the supernatural, and they will always find plenty of it; but to many, also, in an age like this, miracles have been a stumbling-block, and have seemed a reason for rejecting the religion which is made to rest mainly on them... He [Muhammad], at all events, treated the miraculous as subordinate to the moral evidences of His mission, and struck upon a vein of thought and touched a chord of feeling which, it seems to me, is reconcilable at once with the onward march of Science, and all the admitted weaknesses of human nature.[106]

Another factor which vitiated the argument from miracles was the development of secular historical criticism of the Bible and the consequent loss of its authority as an unimpeachable historical source. More specifically, for the "Christian" historian as well as the "non-Christian" historian, by the mid-Victorian period, the Biblical texts were no longer exempt from the process of secular historical inquiry.[107] Thus, the miracles of the New Testament were historically assessable and philosophically assailable, and the contrast between Jesus and Muhammad less striking as a consequence. As the *National Review* put it in 1858, "the historian, who has to deal

---

105 Chadwick, *Secularization*, p. 185.
106 Smith, *Mohammed and Mohammedanism*, pp. 160–3.
107 See Chadwick, *Secularization*, pp. 189–97; see also Reventlow, *The Authority of the Bible*.

simply with matters of fact, can only affirm that every occurrence which comes up to the popular notion of a sign or miracle stands in precisely the same position, whether it is recorded in the gospels or elsewhere... If, then, the absence of miracle can no more detract from the authority of Mahomet than from that of John the Baptist, every other question respecting the founder of Islam, his reforms, his errors, his inspiration and apostleship, must be answered strictly on its own merits..."[108] In short, the presuppositions of science and history rendered unfeasible the argument to the truth of Christianity from miracles, and the argument to the falsity of Islam from their absence. Consequently, one of the main intellectual barriers to a positive assessment of Muhammad and Islam was pushed aside and, as we have seen, intellectual space for alternative images of the Prophet was created.

6. The Night Journey

> Glory be to Him, who carried His servant by night from the Holy Mosque to the Further Mosque the precincts of which We have blessed...
>
> *Quran* 17.1

Of all the miracles imputed to Muhammad, that of his translation from Mecca to Jerusalem was most often commented upon, both by Islamic and by Western commentators.[109] Based on the allusion of Muhammad's translation from Mecca to Jerusalem in the seventeenth Sura of the Quran, later Muslim tradition elaborated the Quranic text into a richly detailed account of Muhammad's journey from Mecca to Jerusalem, and thence to the heavens.

The parameters for the debate during the eighteenth and nineteenth centuries were set by Prideaux on the one hand, and the anonymous author of a life of Muhammad in 1712 on the other. According to Prideaux, Muhammad, in order to satisfy the demands of the people for a miracle, invented the story of his journey to heaven.[110] Prideaux himself was well aware that there were Muslim interpretations of this journey as a vision, the details of which were to be treated figuratively, rather than as a real *physical* translation. But he was probably accurate in his claim that "the major Vote hath carried it for *a real Journey.*"[111] The anonymous author of the

---

108 *National Review,* 1858, p. 154.
109 See Schimmel, *Muhammad,* ch. 9; Widengren, *Muḥammad.*
110 See Prideaux, *The True Nature of Imposture,* p. 52.
111 *Ibid.,* p. 66.

1712 Life held to the other explanation. Aware that Muslims took the journey in a literal sense, and not allegorically[112], he remained unconvinced that Muhammad had perpretrated a deliberate fraud: "I am inclined to think," he wrote, "from his endeavouring to impose such a monstrous story on his Followers, that he was really deceived himself by some Dream or Vision."[113]

In general, interpretations of the night journey reflected already established views of Muhammad's sincerity or duplicity. George Sale, for example, rejected Prideaux's argument that the night journey was contrived by Muhammad to answer expectations among the Meccans of miracles. But he did see it as a contrivance of Muhammad to raise his reputation.[114] His view remained a popular one until the end of the nineteenth century. It was the position adopted in the Life added to the 1757 edition of Ockley's *The History of the Saracens*, it was repeated in the *Encyclopaedia Britannica* in 1817, alluded to in an anonymous life of Muhammad in 1851, and utilised without acknowledgement by Menezes in 1911.[115]

Those most sympathetic to Muhammad preferred, I think, to ignore the issue as much as possible. Consequently, the preponderance of nineteenth century comments are negative. The anonymous author of a 1744 Life, indebted to Prideaux, deliberately and consciously ridiculed the Islamic accounts. "Should it be complained," he concluded, "that I have narrated this journey in a ludicrous manner, my apology is, that, inheriting from nature a satirical turn of mind, and never having met with a subject in the whole compass of my reading which more justly deserved to feel the throngs of ridicule, it was absolutely impossible for me to let it pass with impunity."[116] Charles Mills saw it as a tale well-adapted to the imagination of an ignorant, unphilosophical Arab[117], and William Sime agreed with John Roebuck that the traditional accounts were a "tissue of the most dull and ridiculous absurdities."[118]

Although as early as 1735, it was argued against Prideaux that it was unfair to impute to Muhammad the later wealth of legendary accretions that came to surround the mention in the Quran[119], most critics preferred to ignore or brush the

---

112 See anon., *The Life and Actions of Mahomet*, in *Four Treatises*, p. 55.
113 *Ibid.*, p. 56.
114 Sale, *The Koran*, p. 36.
115 See Ockley, *The History of the Saracens*, p. 25; *Encyclopaedia Britannica*, 1817, xii. 403; anon., *Life of Mohammad*, 1851, p. 42; Menezes, *The Life and Religion of Mahommed*, p. 34.
116 Anon., *The Life of Mahomet*, 1799, p. 48.
117 See Mills, *An History*, p. 17.
118 Sime, *History of Mohammed*, p. 23; see also, *The National Quarterly Review*, 1876, p. 211.
119 See anon., *Reflections on Mohammedism*, 1735, pp. 39–41.

distinction aside. In spite of its awareness of the later development of the story, *The Penny Cyclopaedia* in 1839 imputed much to Muhammad:

> The only miraculous act which Mohammad professed to have accomplished, and which has been greatly exaggerated by his credulous adherents, is a nocturnal journey from the temple of Mecca to Jerusalem, and thence through the heavens, which he pretended to have performed on an imaginary animal like an ass, called Borak...[120]

Even William Muir gave an account which combines the Quran and the tradition though he was fully aware of the minimal Quranic material. However, he did make it clear that, for him, the whole episode was the result of a visionary dream of Muhammad.[121]

Surprisingly perhaps, the night journey was only seldom connected with Muhammad's supposed epilepsy. Still, in 1813, the *Pantologia* did see the night journey, like his other revelations, as a contrivance to explain aways his epilepsy.[122] And Aloys Sprenger viewed it as an effect of the fraudulent behaviour to which most hysterical enthusiasts were prone.[123] But there was one notable instance in the nineteenth century of the interpretation of the night journey as an epileptic experience. Feodor Mikhailovich Dostoievski identified his epileptic experience of God with that of Muhammad:

> All you, healthy people do not even suspect what happiness is, that happiness which we epileptics experience during the second before the attack. In his Koran Mohammed assures us that he saw paradise and was inside. All clever fools are convinced that he is simply a liar and a fraud; Oh no! He is not lying! He really was in paradise during an attack of epilepsy, from which he suffered as I do.[124]

Liar and fraud, sincerely deluded visionary, deceptive hysteric, epileptic prophet – all these images of Muhammad were brought into play in the eighteenth and nineteenth centuries as possible explanations of the night journey.

---

120 *The Penny Cyclopaedia*, 1833, xv. 299; see also anon., *The Life of Mohammed*, 1847, pp. 44–5.
121 Muir, *The Life of Moḥammad*, pp. 121–2.
122 See *Pantologia*, 1813, vii. 144.
123 See Sprenger, *The Life of Mohammed*, pp. 124–5.
124 Quoted by Temkin, *The Falling Sickness*, p. 374; see also Futrell, "Dostoyevsky and Islam."

7. The Profligate Prophet?

According to Norman Daniel, in the West, "Three distinct bodies of fact, the historical details of Muhammad's personal life, the requirements of Islamic sexual ethics and the elements in Paradise which the Qur'ān delineates were linked together to constitute one single theme. Islam was essentially built upon a foundation of sexual licence which was plainly contrary to the natural and the divine law. In one form or another, this opinion has always been part of the Christian attitude to Islam."[125] Daniel's opinion is certainly a valid one until the end of the seventeenth century. Until that time, the image of Muhammad as a voluptuary, and of Islam as a sensual religion was seldom questioned. But from 1700–1900, the question of the sexual propriety of Muhammad, and the licentiousness of Islam was to become a much more complex one. On the one hand, the issue was complicated by better historical knowledge both of the life of Muhammad and changing, more accurate, perceptions of sexual licence in Islam. And, on the other hand, the matter was confused in a Europe liberated from clerical hostility to sensuality, freed to create its own secular image of eastern exoticism, yet bound too by traditional Christian hostility to a religion perceived as promoting sensuality.

Still, as intricate as the issue became during these two hundred years, if we take a broad sweep from 1650 to 1900, although the context obviously varies, there is a continuity in the image of Muhammad as a voluptuary, an image which, as we shall see, even his most ardent defenders were hard put to dispel. In 1678, Thomas Smith linked the sensuality of the Turkish Islam of his day with the profligacy of the Prophet.[126] The author of a 1799 Life declared that Julian the Apostate, Judas Iscariot, Nero, Caligula, and Domitian were pious saints or immaculate angels compared to Muhammad.[127] The author of another Life some fifty years later somewhat coyly omitted a description of the excessive sensuality of Muhammad's habits since no gratification of curiosity could be worth "risking the perpetual shock of the moral feelings of every virtuous mind" which would result.[128] Even Washington Irving, with many qualifications, admitted that, in some respects, Muhammad was a voluptuary.[129] Aloys Sprenger gave putative scientific validation to the traditional portrait of Muhammad's sexual appetites. Noting that one of the

125 Daniel, *Islam and the West*, p. 152.
126 Smith, *Remarks*, pp. 28–9; see also Jenkin, *The Reasonableness and Certainty of the Christian Religion*, p. 443; Herbert, *Some Years Travels*, p. 337.
127 Anon., *The Life of Mahomet*, 1799, p. 81.
128 Anon., *The Life of Mohammed*, 1847, p. xiv.
129 Irving, *Life of Mahomet*, p. 231; see also anon., *Life of Mohammad*, 1851, pp. 120, 123.

symptoms of hysteria was nymphomania, he concluded that Muhammad's "compulsive inclination to voluptuousness was a symptom of his illness and that he suffered from impotent Satyriasm."[130] And Koelle suggested in 1889 that the Prophet's death was caused by the unrestrained sensuality in which he had indulged, a sensuality that had undermined his constitution and ruined his nervous system.[131]

In the medieval image of Islam, sexual permissiveness had often been seen as extending to homosexuality, with the blessing of Muhammad. Some had argued that it extended even to bestiality and incest. As late as 1593, Henrie Smith in his *Gods Arrovve against Atheists,* a compilation of virtually all the possible negative portraits of the Prophet, accused him of committing "buggerie with an Asse..."[132] Fortunately, such claims did not survive the end of the sixteenth century. Although eighteenth and nineteenth century writers did not often ascribe the endorsement of homosexuality to Muhammad, the attribution of it to men in Islamic cultures still occurred. In 1704, for example, Joseph Pitts, an English sailor captured by Algerian pirates and finally set free after making the pilgrimage to Mecca, remarked that "'Tis common for Men there to fall in love with Boys, as 'tis here in England to be in love with women."[133] Robert Beverley in 1829 maintained that sodomy had become the great distinctive mark of the Muslim character.[134] And Trowbridge in 1882, in his vindictive account of the Turks, suggested that the propensity of the Turks for "the crime against nature" could be laid at Muhammad's door.[135]

But it was Muhammad's purported penchant for heterosexual activity that was the central focus of criticism and that which his defenders had to rebut. One aspect of this was the Western assumption that he had gained the affection of his wife Khadija through sorcery. In 1652, for example, Peter Heylyn in his *Cosmographie* maintained that Muhammad gained the hand of Khadija through his sorcery, as well as his personal comeliness and his business acumen,[136] although by 1679 the accusation of sorcery was rejected by Addison in favour of Muhammad's carefulness in business matters.[137]

Again, such a myth did not survive into a more critically aware eighteenth century. On the contrary, the knowledge that Muhammad had lived a life of faithful

---

130 Sprenger, *Das Leben,* i. 209.
131 See Koelle, *Mohammed and Mohammedanism,* p. 229.
132 Smith, *Gods Arrovve,* ch. iv.
133 Pitts, *A True and Faithful Account,* ch. iii.
134 Beverley, *A Letter to Godfrey Higgins,* p. 34.
135 Trowbridge, "Mohammedanism," p. 283; see also Palgrave, *Narrative,* i. 434–5.
136 See Heylyn, *Cosmographie,* p. 121; see also Babington, *Polychronicon,* p. 23; anon., *A Lytell Treatise,* iii.
137 Addison, *The Life and Death of Mahumed,* p. 16.

constancy with Khadija until her death became a major argument against his assumed profligacy. The author of *Reflections on Mohammedism* in 1735 remarked upon the extraordinary degree of continence demonstrated by Muhammad in remaining monogamous:

> Could it, do ye think, have been any Scandal for him to have marry'd other Women, when almost every Man in the Country had a Number of Wives?... To what are we then to impute this great Temperance and Sobriety? Was it Chastity? Was it Virtue? Was it Gratitude in a Man so naturally fired at the Sight of a beautiful Object? It must certainly have been something of the Kind.[138]

His monogamous relationship with Khadija was to constitute the main defence against the assusation of Muhammad's essential voluptuousness until the end of the nineteenth century.[139]

But as we shall see later, his actions after the death of Khadija were not to be so easily defended. Moreover, for those convinced of Muhammad's essentially sensual nature, his faithfulness to Khadija could be explained away. Joseph White, in 1785 for example, argued that Muhammad had merely concealed his sensuality until he had gained power.[140] The author of a 1799 Life argued, from the fact that the Prophet later married younger women, that his faithful marriage to Khadija was merely a cynical exercise in political ambition.[141] For Koelle in 1889, always inclined to decry Muhammad as weak-minded, his constancy was merely the consequence of Khadija's strength and wisdom: "she succeeded in keeping him from marrying any other wife as long as she lived, though at her death, when he had long ceased to be a young man, he indulged without restraint in the multiplication of wives."[142]

During the medieval and early modern periods, Muhammad's polygamy after the death of Khadija – at the end of his life he had some nine wives – reinforced the image of Muhammad's profligacy and the licentious nature of Islam. But the traditional criticism became a little muted in the eighteenth century. As Norman Daniel explains, "The supposed Islamic sexuality, which had been a point of particular repugnance to a world under clerical guidance, and remained so to the

138 Anon., *Refections on Mohammedism*, 1735, p. 12.
139 See e.g., *British Quarterly Review*, 1872, pp. 129–30; *The Quarterly Review*, 1877, p. 215; Lane-Poole, *Studies*, pp. 77–9; see also Schimmel, *Muhammad*, pp. 49–50 for the same defence.
140 See White, *Sermons*, p. 105.
141 See, anon., *The Life of Mahomet*, 1799, pp. 11–12.
142 Koelle, *Mohammed and Mohammedanism*, p. 47; see also Menezes, *The Life and Religion of Mahommed*, pp. 13–14.

pious, became a positive attraction to a new public... Harsh judgements were mitigated by the growing attraction of exotic Ways."[143]

But there was more to the interest in polygamy than merely a fascination with the exotic East. It was grounded in social issues of significance in eighteenth century England. It was proposed, for example, as a solution to the large surplus of women, and questions were asked about its being preferable to divorce. Serious supporters of polygamy based their advocacy on the Mosaic Law and the Law of Nature. Deists defended it by reference to the example of the Old Testament Patriarchs (though partly merely to ridicule Scripture); and Hume saw it merely as a matter of social and political custom.[144]

The argument from natural law played a role in discussions of Islamic polygamy. In the 1670's, Stubbe saw polygamy as evidence of Muhammad's great wisdom as a legislator: "The Alcoran gives liberty to each Musulman to take to himself wives two, three, or four, as he pleaseth, except he fear he is not able to render to them all due benevolence. Wherein the doctrine of Mahomet doth exactly agree with the Law of Nature, except that he puts a positive restraint in his Law to a determinate Number..."[145] Boulainvilliers in 1731 saw Muslim polygamy as the result either of Muhammad's fondness for women, or as "the consequence of that regard which every wise legislator must have for particular and popular customs that do not interfere with the law of nature."[146] George Sale defended Muhammàd as merely following the customs of his time, and as copying Old Testament precedents: "The several laws relating to marriages and divorces, and the peculiar privileges granted to Mohammed in his Korān, were almost taken by him from the Jewish decisions...; and therefore he might think those institutions the more just and reasonable, as he found them practised or approved by the professors of a religion which was confessedly of divine original."[147]

A further rational explanation of polygamy which provided some defense for Muhammad was that from the nature of climate. The sensuality of the Muslim Paradise, of Muhammad, indeed of Islamic male sensuality in general were often seen as the product of the Arabian climate. Prideaux himself was heir to the Classical tradition of the relationship between temperature and temperament.[148] According to Prideaux, Muhammad's view of Paradise answered the carnal desires of the Arabians: "For they being within the torrid zone were, through the nature of

---

143 Daniel, *Islam, Europe and Empire*, p. 23.
144 See Owen, "Polygamy and Deism"; Watt, *The Rise of the Novel*, pp. 166–7.
145 Stubbe, *An Account*, p. 172.
146 Boulainvilliers, *The Life of Mahomet*, p. 172.
147 Sale, *The Koran*, p. 31.
148 See Glacken, *Traces on the Rhodian Shore*.

the clime, as well as the excessive corruption of their manner exceedingly given to the love of women..."[149]

But the same argument was turned against Prideaux in 1720. Omar criticised Prideaux's claim that Muhammad's polygamy was evidence of his lust, both on grounds of custom, and climate. Prideaux, wrote Omar,

> is born in a cold Country, and because the Laws and Customs of that place oblige the Husband to have but one Wife, he attributes the more to a sinful Lust, thó it has always been a Use in most of the hotter countries, to have a plurality of Wives; and Nature itself seems to have established this; for whereas there are more Males than Females born in a colder Climate, there are more Females than Males born in these regions nearer the Sun.[150]

Such forms of argument perhaps reached their pinnacle in 1748 in the Baron de Montesquieu's *De l'Esprit des lois*. In hot climates, he argued, women mature sexually at an age earlier than they attain maturity in reason; thus, conditions are favourable for male dominance and polygamy. In temperate climes, however, women's maturity, sexually and rationally, parallels that of men; and therefore, there is more sexual equality and monogamy. For Montesquieu, this partly explained why Islam had been so successful in Asia but not in Europe, and Christianity in Europe but not in Asia.[151] William Paley was able to explain in terms of climate not only the Islamic propensity to sensuality, but also the reason for its prohibition on alcohol. In hotter climates, declared Paley, the appetite of the sexes is ardent, the passion for alcohol moderate. Thus, "In compliance with this distinction, although Mahomet laid a restraint upon the drinking of wine, in the use of women he allowed an almost unbounded indulgence..."[152]

Nineteenth century writers were less rationalistic than their predecessors on the matter of polygamy. Certainly, they were more censorious. Some, like the Utilitarian Perronet Thompson, condemned it on social grounds. Monogamy in the West had resulted in single-mindedness; the Muslim had dissipated his energies among "a quaternion of slaves."[153] Throughout the nineteenth century, there was an awareness that Islam did not endorse sexual libertinism. But there was a perception that Islam, in spite of its strict controls on sexuality, had legitimated promiscuity.

---

149 Prideaux, *The True Nature of Imposture*, p. 25; see also *Pantologia*, 1813, vii. 143; anon., *The History of Mahomet*, 1821, p. 17.
150 *Miscellanea Aurea*, p. 170.
151 See Glacken, *Traces on the Rhodian Shore*, pp. 573–4.
152 Paley, *The Works*, p. 408; see also Porteus, *A Summary*, p. 72.
153 Thompson, "Arabs and Persians," p. 224; see also Daniel, *Islam, Europe and Empire*, pp. 36–48. In what follows, I cite in the main only sources not utilized by Daniel.

Women, for example, were seen as the victims of a legally-sanctioned system of oppression. Victorian men waxed moralistically and often a little self-righteously. As *The Dublin Review* put it in 1839, "And what is in fine this rigid external discipline – this veiling and this separation – this prohibition of all intercourse with other men, which the Koran imposes upon women? What else is it but the hollow caricature of chastity?"[154] Many saw the institution of polygamy and the seclusion of women as tantamount to slavery. As a result of early marriages, complained the author of a Life in 1847, Muslim women become their husbands' slaves.[155] *The North British Review* for 1855 declared that a licenced polygamy degraded the whole female sex: "she becomes at once an inferior being, a creature created for his pleasure,... in a word she becomes a slave."[156] Such criticisms were not unreasonable, though the imputation that they had originated with Muhammad was. Neither the veiling of women nor their seclusion are to be found in the Quran. Moreover, Victorian men, alert to the plight of women in some Islamic cultures, were not so attuned to that of women in their own. As John Stuart Mill was to write in 1869 in his *Subjection of Women*, "The wife is the actual bond-servant of her husband: no less so, as far as legal obligation goes, than slaves commonly so called."[157]

To be sure, there were defenders of the harem who emphasised its bourgeois nature. For David Urquhart, the harem was "the concentration in one spot of security, protection, filial duties, paternal authority, love, delicacy of manners, and of intercourse."[158] But these were the exceptions. Generally, in the literature on Islam as a religion, criticism remained the norm. Bosworth Smith maintained that Muhammad had improved the lot of women. But he felt he had to admit that the institution of the harem had excluded women from exercising the humanising, spiritualising influence on men which they had done in Christendom. Morever, he argued, the life of the Harem was not congenial to the development of the finer qualities of the human soul: "Triviality, selfishness, heart-burnings, deadly hatreds, if nothing worse, are the weeds which must, in the nature of things... find in it a congenial soil."[159] Smith and Trowbridge disagreed on most issues about Islam; but on this they agreed although Trowbridge was typically more scathing. "The 'harem,'" he wrote, "so sacredly secluded from the world, is the nursery of impure desires, the home of vile gossip; its atmosphere is tainted with pollution. Turkish women, excluded as they are from the society of men, learn to think of all

154 *The Dublin Review*, 1839, p. 106; see also Döllinger, *Muhammeds Religion*, p. 20.
155 See anon., *The Life of Mohammed*, 1847, pp. 146–7.
156 *The North British Review*, 1855, p. 463.
157 Quoted by Gay, *The Bourgeois Experience*, i. 175.
158 Urquhart, *The Spirit of the East*, i. 410.
159 Smith, *Mohammed and Mohammedanism*, p. 255.

intercourse with the opposite sex as low and degrading, and this conviction or sentiment works like a moral poison at the very source of family and social life."[160]

Polygamy was also viewed as one element in the Eastern inability socially to progress. Polygamy, divorce, slavery – all kept Islamic societies from adapting to modernity and change. In 1895, for example, G. M. Grant concluded that a religion "that treats woman not as the helpmeet, but as the slave or plaything of man, cannot be permanent. It must pass away... It is at war with the fundamental principles, tendencies, and customs of modern life, and with all that is best and purest in the heart of humanity."[161] Or as Edward Palmer succinctly put it, "One of the greatest blots on El Islām is that it keeps the women in a state of degradation, and therefore effectually prevents the progress of any race professing the religion."[162]

No nineteenth century writer on Islam endorsed polygamy as a viable alternative to monogamy. But those who were sympathetic to Muhammad tended to argue that he was to be praised for limiting it. Many saw him as a reformer of a prior greater evil, and as having generally improved the position of women in Arabic society. In 1834, for example, Sismondi noted that before the time of Muhammad, the Arabs had enjoyed unbounded licence in love and marriage, Muhammad, he went on to say, forbade incest, punished adultery, and diminished the facility of divorce.[163] Bosworth Smith's apology was typical: "As a true Arab, Mohammed recognised polygamy as an existing institution; as a reforming legislator, he made many regulations for lessening its evils; but it is hardly more fair on these grounds to say that Mohammedanism is responsible for polygamy, than it is to say that Christianity is responsible for slavery."[164] And Smith found supporters in the *Dublin University Magazine* in 1876, *The Quarterly Review* in 1877, and *The Dublin Review* in 1878.[165]

There were even a few commentators who wanted to deny outright that Muhammad was a voluptuary. Prime, among these was Carlyle. He, like others, emphasised Muhammad's ascetic life-style.[166] Similarly, Stanley Lane-Poole declared that

160 Trowbridge, "Mohammedanism," p. 286.
161 Grant, *The Religions of the World*, p. 49; see also Davies, "Mohammed," p. 331; Johnstone, *Muhammad and his Power*, p. 157.
162 Palmer, *The Qur'ān*, p. lxxv.
163 See Sismondi, *History*, i. 293–4; see also Freeman, *History and Conquest of the Saracens*, pp. 52–3.
164 Smith, *Mohammed and Mohammedanism*, p. 199; but cf. Badger, "Mohammed," p. 97.
165 See *Dublin University Magazine*, 1876, p. 144; *The Quarterly Review*, 1877, p. 227; *The Dublin Review*, 1878, p. 423; see also Grant, *The Religions of the World*, p. 35; but cf. Dods, *Mohammed*, p. 54.
166 See Carlyle, *On Heroes*, p. 71.

Muhammad was no voluptuary: "The simple austerity of his daily life, to the very last, his hard mat for sleeping on, his plain food, his self-imposed menial work, point him out as an ascetic rather than a voluptuary in most senses of the word."[167] Meredith Townsend in 1861 admitted that he was, in his later years, a man who loved women, but he rejected the term "licentious." Though good and bad are recorded of Muhammad, he suggested, "we hear of no seduction, no adultery, no interference with the families of his followers."[168]

But such arguments, cogent as they were, did not take into account what remained for many the crucial indicator of the Prophets sensuality. This was his own abrogation of his limit of four wives. However constant he had been with Khadija, however ascetic his lifestyle, however much he had reformed prior evils of polygamy and female infanticide, this abrogation allowed the image of Muhammad's profligacy to maintain itself throughout the nineteenth century.

Humphrey Prideaux saw it as an aspect of his cynical imposture: "Whatever Laws he gave to restrain the Lust of other Men, he took care always to except himself, resolving it seems to take his full swing herein without Let or Controul, according as the violent bent of his brutish Appetite this way, should lead him."[169] And a century later, in 1800, Beilby Porteus compared Muhammad who "laid claim to a special permission from heaven to riot in the most unlimited sensuality" with Jesus who was "perfectly holy and undefiled."[170] Such arguments occurred throughout the nineteenth century. The feeling of the author of the Religious Tract Society's Life in 1847 was not untypical: "To present such a compound of iniquities, in connexion with the pretence of a religion from heaven, is to sicken the heart."[171] As *The Quarterly Review* for 1877 remarked, all Bosworth Smith's ingenuity was taxed in defending this aspect of the life of Muhammad.[172] Of Muhammad's relaxation of his own teaching on polygamy, even Smith conceded, "it is a blot, and, in the Christian view, an indelible blot, upon his memory..."[173]

But we must not over-estimate the significance of these criticism of Muhammad's taking more wives than he allowed others to take. For the overall picture of Muhammad's purported profligacy is a vastly more multi-layered one during the

---

167 Lane-Poole, *Studies*, p. 77.
168 *National Review*, 1861, p. 339.
169 Prideaux, *The True Nature of Imposture*, p. 149; see also Addison, *The Life and Death of Mahumed*, pp. 26–7; Bayle, *Historical and Critical Dictionary*, ii. 251.
170 Porteus, *A Summary*, p. 68.
171 Anon., *The Life of Mohammed*, 1847, p. 63; see also Green, *The Life of Mahomet*, pp. 216–7; anon., *Life of Mohammed*, 1851, pp. 79–80.
172 See *The Quarterly Review*, 1877, p. 217.
173 Smith, *Mohammed and Mohammedanism*, p. 114.

nineteenth century than the rather crude picture of sensuality presented by Voltaire in 1742 or Prideaux in 1697. Muhammad is by no means the ideal hero pictured by Islam itself, but neither is he the satanic heretic of the Christian myth. If nothing else, in both their praise and blame, the Victorians had created an historical figure and drawn a very human portrait of the Prophet.

Chapter Three

The Prophet and the Book

1. The Conspiracy and the Book

> Good reader, the great Arabian impostor, now at
> last, after a thousand years, is, by way of
> France, arrived in England, and his Alcoran, or
> Gallimaufry of Errors (a Brat as deformed as
> the Parent, and as full of Heresies as his scald Head
> was of scurf) hath learned to speak English.[1]

Such was the way in which the Quran, the sacred text of Islam, was introduced to readers of the first English translation in 1649 by Alexander Ross. The year of King Charles's execution, it was a time of religious ferment in England. And Ross therefore found it necessary to write an admonition to assure his readers that it was no more dangerous to read the Quran than to read works of heretical Christian sects, or books on palmistry, astrology, or necromancy. Still, he wanted to argue, only those of a strong faith should read the Quran; and "weak, ignorant, inconstant, and disaffected minds to the Truth, must not venture to meddle with this unhallowed piece, lest they be polluted with the touch thereof."[2]

Moreover, Ross's account of the origin of the Quran was quite in agreement with the traditional polemic against the work, namely, that it was a forgery concocted by Muhammad with the assistance of others. According to him the Quran was "a misshapen issue of Mahomet's brain, being brought forth by the help of no other midwifery than of a *Jew* and a *Nestorian*, making use of a tame Pigeon (which he had taught to pick corn out of his Ears) instead of the holy Ghost and causing silly people to believe, that in his falling sickness... he had conference with the Angel *Gabriel*."[3]

The general belief that the Quran was a forgery formulated by the Prophet from diverse sources, particularly the Jewish and Christian scriptures, underlaid the various specific legends constructed in the West – legends which survived into the nineteenth century – to explain the Quran and to discredit Muhammad. Most

---

1 Du Ryer, *The Alcoran*, pp. 409–10.
2 Quoted by Smith, *Islam in English Literature*, p. 29.
3 *Ibid.*, p. 28.

popular of these legends was that Muhammad was assisted in the composition of the Quran by an heretical Christian and a Jew.

The legend of the conspiracy between Muhammad and his Christian accomplice probably has its origin in the Muslim biographical tradition of the life of Muhammad. According to this, Muhammad at the age of nine or twelve accompanied a Meccan caravan to Syria. The Christian hermit Bahira there recognized the young Muhammad as a future prophet by means of certain miraculous signs, in particular, the "seal of of prophecy" between his shoulders.[4] The legend was developed in Byzantine Christendom to discredit Muhammad's claim to have received the Quran from God by inspiration. Bahira, or Sergius as he became most commonly known in the West, instructed Muhammad in the Scriptures, and schooled him in how best to advance his claims to prophethood.[5] Later, in the twelfth century, Petrus Alfonsi, a Spanish Jew converted to Christianity, expanded the legend of Sergius to include the idea that Muhammad had also been instructed by an heretical Jew.[6]

These two legends, that of the heretical Christian and that of the heretical Jew assisting Muhammad in the composition of the Quran, were a commonplace in Elizabethan England. We read, for example, in the 1572 collection of Muenster's *Cosmographye* that Muhammad "began to make a newe Lawe by the healpe of his mayster Sergius and certain Jewes his companions, borrowing some things of the Hebrewes, and some things of the christiās [sic] discipline..."[7] George Whetstones in 1586 repeated the legend that Sergius had fled from Constantinople to Arabia because of his heresy.[8] And Henrie Smith in 1593 saw Satan as having furnished Muhammed not only with a Jew and with Sergius, but also with another abominable heretic, one John of Antioch.[9]

The legends were still very much alive in the England of Alexander Ross. In 1609, for example, William Biddulph wrote of Muhammad's being assisted by Sergius an Arian, John a Nestorian, and a Talmudic Jew.[10] George Sandys claimed in 1608 that Muhammad compiled the Quran in a cave over some two years with the assistance of Sergius a Nestorian, and Abdalla a Jew.[11] We find them too in the life of

---

4 See *The Encyclopaedia of Islam*, i. 922–3.
5 See also Chew, *The Crescent and the Rose*, p. 402, where Chew sees the Sergius legend as a combination of two Muslim traditions, that of Bahira, and that of Waraqah, the teacher of Muhammad.
6 See Metlitzki, *The Matter of Araby*, p. 20.
7 Muenster, *Cosmographye*, p. 64.
8 See Whetstones, *The English Myrror*, p. 55.
9 See Smith, *Gods Arrovve*, ch. 4.
10 See Biddulph, *The Travels*, p. 50.
11 Sandys, *Travailes*, p. 40.

Muhammad ascribed to Walter Raleigh in 1637, in William Lithgow in 1614, in Thomas Coryat in 1618, in Peter Heylyn in 1652, in Thomas Herbert in 1665, in Thomas Smith in 1678, in Richard Knolles in 1687, and in the many editions of Alexander Ross's *Pansebeia*.[12] In virtually all of these cases, the legends are cited with the purpose of decrying Islam as a mere hodgepodge of previously existing religions and thus destroying its claims to any originality. As Prideaux summed it up in 1697, "For his *Religion* being made up of three parts, whereof one was borrowed from the *Jews*, another from the *Christians*, and the third from the *Heathen Arabs*, Abdollah furnished the first of them, *Bahira* the second, and *Mahomet* himself the last; so that there was no need of any other help to compleat the *Imposture*."[13]

A more critical approach to the legends however may be found among several early eighteenth century authors. Already in the 1670's, Henry Stubbe had expressed serious doubts about their historicity, and, indeed, had made a number of reasonable counter arguments. Apart from the fact that there appeared no Abdallah a Jew, or Sergius a Nestorian in the Islamic tradition, Stubbe suggested that the religious mix in the Arabia of the time of the prophet gave him "occasion and opportunity to examine and try all Sects and Sorts of Religions."[14] Moreover, he argued, the Quran was not composed in a desert prior to Muhammad's apostleship, but published on such occasions when the need arose, mostly at Medina, "where, having so many eyes upon him, he could not have had any such Assistance in any private manner but it would have given suspicion and umbrage in that City amongst his followers and so near confidents and secretaries as he there retained about him; or had the pretended Sergius and Abdalla appeared publicly, their names had certainly been recorded by the Mahometans amongst the principal Doctors of their Law and Propagators of their Religion."[15]

For the seventeenth century, Stubbe's views were exceptional, and those of Prideaux more the norm. But Prideaux's position too was to come under attack in the *Miscellanea Aurea* in 1720. For Abdulla Mahumed Omar, that Muhammad had been accused by his enemies of receiving help from others, as Prideaux had pointed out, was quite insufficient to prove that Sergius and Abdollah were the accomplices. Moreover, he declared not unreasonably, the accusation of Muhammad's enemies that he had had assistance could not be taken as proof of such. Jesus cast out devils

---

12 See Raleigh, *The Life and Death of Mahomet*, pp. 10–11; Lithgow, *A Most Delectable and True Discourse*, no p. no.'s; Coryat, *Mr. Thomas Coriat to his Friends*, no p. no.'s; Heylyn, *Cosmographie*, p. 121; Herbert, *Some Years Travels*, p. 337; Smith, *Remarks*, p. 53; Knolles, *The Turkish History*, p. 49; Ross, *Pansebeia*, p. 162.
13 Prideaux, *The True Nature of Imposture*, p. 47; see also pp. 48–9.
14 Stubbe, *An Account*, p. 144.
15 *Ibid.*, pp. 145–6.

by Beelzebub according to *his* enemies, "yet sure this Author [i. e. Prideaux] will not allow those blasphemies against that holy One, to be sufficient Fact for any Enemy to insert as Truth, in any History he should think fit to write of the Life of that Prophet of the Christians."[16] Boulainvilliers too remained unconvinced. After suggesting that the legend of Sergius was merely a Christian embellishment of the Islamic tradition about Bahira, he concluded that the whole tale was too improbable to be credible.[17] The *Cyclopaedia* in 1738 also did not endorse the Sergius legend although, like Stubbe, it suggested that the many heretics in the Arabia of Muhammad's time "furnished the impostor with passages, and crude ill-conceived doctrines out of the Scriptures..."[18] And similarly, George Sale, in 1734, was sceptical of the value of the reports by Christian writers of the assistance that Muhammad received, though he deemed it highly probable that the Prophet had received much assistance from others, "as his countrymen failed not to object to him."[19]

The objections of such as Stubbe, Omar, and Boulainvilliers were generally ignored, although on occasion, while the legend was repeated, its intention was changed to rebound to Muhammad's credit. Thus, for example, in 1796, Thomas Alcock saw Fergius [sic] and Muhammad as cooperating to form a monotheistic religion that would embrace all parties, Pagans, Jews, and Christians. His means were dubious, but the perceived end a noble one. Muhammad, claimed Alcock, "was very sincere in his attempt to establish this principle, and to throw down idolatry... This true principle, so agreeable to human reason, easily gained admittance with the wise and considerate..."[20] And, on occasion too, the legend was changed better to fit known facts in the life of the Prophet. Thus, for example, in an anonymous life of Muhammad in 1815, the legend of Sergius and the forgery of the Quran were transposed to the Muslim tradition of Bahira: "materials for the composition of it (were) sent to Mahomet from the monk... by the means of caravans continually passing and re-passing between Mecca and Bosra."[21]

Be that as it may, the legend in its original form and with its original polemical intention, survived through the nineteenth century, especially in more popular writings. The story of the conspiracy between Muhammad and his various accomplices occurred, for example, in an anonymous Life in 1799, in *The English Encyclopaedia* in 1802, in the *Pantologia* in 1813, in the *Encyclopaedia Perthensis* in 1816, and in the *Encyclopaedia Britannica* in 1842 under the respective entries on

16 *Miscellanea Aurea*, p. 169.
17 Boulainvilliers, *The Life of Mahomet*, p. 205; see also pp. 240–3.
18 *Cyclopaedia*, 1738, "Alcoran."
19 Sale, *The Koran*, p. 49; see also *Encyclopaedia Britannica*, 1771, iii. 11.
20 Alcock, *The Rise of Mahomet*, p. 21.
21 Anon., *Life and Actions of Mahomet*, 1815, pp. 7–8.

"Mohammedanism."[22] It was endorsed also by William van Mildert in 1806, by George Akehurst in 1859, by *The National Quarterly Review* in 1876, by Koelle in 1889, and by Menezes in 1911.[23] And a few popular writers, dependent on Prideaux in the main for their information, continued to repeat the Byzantine tradition that Muhammad, having made use of his monastic accomplice, had him murdered.[24]

To be sure, among the many nineteenth century authors sympathetic to Islam, these legends were either explicitly rejected or, more generally, ignored. But they did survive for a longer period than several other legends of Byzantine origin which had to do with the promulgation of the Quran: that of the dove or pidgeon trained by Muhammad to eat grain from his ear, and then exhibited to the people as the Holy Ghost in the act of inspiring him; and that of the ox (or cow, or camel, or ass) with the Quran hung about its neck, or fastened to its horns, and trained to bring the heavenly messages to Muhammad while preaching.

These legends were a familiar part of anti-Muslim polemic in both sixteenth and seventeenth century England. Muenster, Smith, Sandys, Wybarne, Coryat, Heylyn, and Herbert, all made reference to them.[25] Most importantly, they were included in the life of Muhammad appended to the first English translation of the Quran in 1649: "as a Pigeon being taught by him to come and pick a Pease out of his ear, he told them it was the Holy Ghost that came to tel him what God would have him do; so an Ox brought him a Chapter of the *Alcoran* upon his horns, in a full assembly."[26]

But virtually in the same year, the legend of the dove had been rejected by the Arabist Edward Pococke in his *Specimen historiae Arabum*. The story had been perpetuated by Hugo Grotius in his *De Veritate Religionis Christianae*. Pococke, while translating this work into Arabic for missionary purposes, obtained an admission from Grotius that it had no Islamic authority, and consequently deleted it from his Arabic translation.[27] Henry Stubbe, following Pococke, rejected the

22 See anon., *The Life of Mahomet*, 1799, pp. 97–8; *The English Encyclopaedia*, 1802, v. 470; *Pantologia*, 1813, vii. 144; *Encyclopaedia Perthensis*, 1816, xiii. 576; *The Encyclopaedia Britannica*, 1842, xiv. 32.
23 See van Mildert, *Infidelity*, i. 205; Akehurst, *Imposture Instanced*, p. 8; *The National Quarterly Review*, 1876, p. 204; Koelle, *Mohammed and Mohammedanism*, p. 84; Menezes, *The Life and Religion of Mahommed*, p. 163.
24 See Prideaux, *The True Nature of Imposture*, pp. 36–7; Sime, *History of Mohammed*, pp. 15–16; anon., *The Life of Mahomet*, 1799, p. 102; Akehurst, *Imposture Instanced*, pp. 13–14; and cf. Green, *The Life of Mahomet*, p. 69.
25 See Muenster, *Cosmographye*, p. 64; Smith, *Gods Arrovve*, ch. iv; Sandys, *Travailes*, p. 42; Wybarne, *The New Age*, p. 95; Coryat, *Mr. Thomas Coriat to his Friends*, no p. no.; Heylyn, *Cosmographie*, p. 121; Herbert, *Some Years Travels*, p. 337.
26 Du Ryer, *The Alcoran*, p. 406.
27 See Holt, "The Study of Arabic Historians," p. 451.

story of the pidgeon and along with it, that of the ox as Christian fabrications.[28] Even Prideaux rejected both legends as "idle tales not to be credited."[29] And a short time later, Joseph Pitts, drawing on his quite unique first-hand experience of Islam, declared that the story of the pidgeon had no currency among Muslims.[30]

Effectively, these legends disappeared from anti-Muslim polemic from this time. Even the virulent anti-Muslim Life published in 1799 called them "such palpable absurdities ... that they never would have been practiced by a sagacious deceiver," and went on to argue that they were Christian inventions.[31] Support for the legends is virtually absent from nineteenth century writings. Only in one instance, in an 1815 Life, is the legend of the pidgeon mentioned; but even here it is merely added to the main body of the text as an afterthought.[32]

2. The Prophetic Potpourri

By the Victorian period, then, the legends of the pidgeon and the ox had disappeared, and the legends of Muhammad's accomplices, in spite of the authority of Prideaux, were fading. But the principle underlying them – that the Quran was discredited by being merely a potpourri of the writings and traditions of religions which existed before Islam – remained. Although seldom accused of conspiracy to defraud with the help from others, Muhammad was still often seen as a mere syncretistic plagiariser, desiring to be all things to all men.

Thus, for example, Joseph White in 1785 saw Muhammad as concocting a religion which, by flattering the corrupt passions and prejudices of Christian, idolater and Jew might embrace each of these. The materials of the Quran, he argued, "are wholly borrowed from the Jewish and Christian scriptures, from the Talmudical legends and apocryphal gospels then current in the East, and from the traditions and fables which abounded in Arabia."[33] And Beilby Porteus, Bishop of London, declared in 1800 that the Quran had little novelty or originality to recommend it, it being mainly borrowed from the Old and New Testaments;

---

28 See Stubbe, *An Account*, pp. 150–1.
29 Prideaux, *The True Nature of Imposture*, p. 48.
30 Pitts, *A True and Faithful Account*, Preface.
31 Anon., *The Life of Mahomet*, 1799, p. 162.
32 See anon., *Life and Actions of Mahomet*, 1815, p. 31.
33 White, *Sermons*, p. 162.

although he went on to suggest that, because the imposter vitiated and debased everything he touched, the Biblical sources were hardly recognizable.[34]

For many who saw Muhammad still as the imposter, Muhammad's blending of previous writings into the Quran was only another aspect of this. And in general, as we shall see in more detail later, attitudes to the Quran were, in most cases, merely the reflection of a prior judgement on the character of the Prophet. Thus, a popular Life of the Prophet in 1821 saw the Quran as a medley of Judaism, Christian heresies, and Arabian paganism drawn up to meet Muhammad's ambitious designs.[35] The same argument was put by David Williamson in 1824 in his *Reflections on the Four Principal Religions*, and by Edward Upham in 1829.[36] For Charles Forster, in the same year, the elements of Judaism and Christianity incorporated into the Quran did betray some marks and tokens of their divine original, albeit disguised and desecrated. But this suggested to Forster that the Quran was merely an anti-Christian parody of the Jewish and Christian scriptures: "It is not until we shall have thoroughly sifted the gold from the dross, the mutilated fragments of divine truth, from the refuse mass in which they lie buried and embedded, that the impious fabricator of this lying revelation can stand forth discovered to the light; bearing the stamp of antichrist upon his forehead!"[37]

That Muhammad had incorporated Jewish and Christian writings into the Quran seldom rebounded to his credit. The *Foreign Quarterly Review* in 1833 noted that, not only was there no novelty in the Quran because it had been formed from Judaism, Christianity and Zoroastrianism, but also that Muhammad seemed only to have consulted the corrupt portions of each.[38] The *Pantologia* in 1813 characterized the Quran as "as compound of sublime truths, of incredible tales, and ludicrous events,"[39] while the Baptist Samuel Green declared the Quran owed everything to Scripture "except its spirit, its manifest contradictions, its puerile follies, and its superstition."[40] Dean Milman went further. "Even Mohammedan fable," he exclaimed, "had none of the inventive originality of fiction."[41]

Even those sympathetic to Muhammad did not find any originality in the Quran, although they variously tried to defend it. William Taylor for example, in 1834

---

34 Porteus, *A Summary*, p. 81.
35 See anon., *The History of Mahomet*, 1821, p. 7.
36 See Williamson, *Reflections on the Four Principal Religions*, i. 82; Upham, *History*, i. 30.
37 Forster, *Mahometanism Unveiled*, ii. 76; see also *The Edinburgh Review*, 1829–30, pp. 335–6.
38 *The Foreign Quarterly Review*, 1833, p. 197.
39 *Pantologia*, 1813, vii. 144.
40 Green, *The Life of Mahomet*, p. 149.
41 Milman, *History*, ii. 10–11.

viewed the Quran as a vast plagiarism – "a booty, rather than the fair fruit of mental labour."[42] But he argued nonetheless that the Quran was evidence, not of a vulgar imposter but of an elevated and impassioned soul:

> If, on the rich fields of sacred literature, he
> plundered – he plundered like a prince. The spoil
> which he gathered so largely from the Jewish and
> Christian Scriptures might be likened to that
> with which certain learned and magnificent conquerors
> have graced their triumphs – they have indeed
> trampled upon and overthrown the ancient seats of
> arts and learning; but yet have first snatched
> from the devastations of war each signal
> moment of greatness and beauty.[43]

Frederick Maurice saw Muhammad's lack of originality as a virtue. A teacher, he explained, may exercise a greater power by reviving the old than by inventing the new.[44] Similarly, *The Eclectic Magazine* for 1858 saw the Quran, judged by any European standards, as a cumbersome mass of legend with a monotonous recurrence of common-place thoughts and precepts. But it did recognize that Arabian standards of literary excellence were different, and moreover, that "A revelation, to be genuine, need not be entirely dissimilar to those which have preceded it."[45] Bosworth Smith too wondered whether lack of originality was any reproach to a religion. But he went further than most of his contemporaries in stressing the creative genius of the Prophet, irrespective of the sources of much of the Quran. In the Quran, he maintained, "we have a mirror of one of the master-spirits of the world; often inartistic, incoherent, self contradictory, dull, but impregnated with a few grand ideas which stand out from the whole; a mind seething with the inspiration pent within it, 'intoxicated with God,' but full of human weaknesses, from which he never pretended – and it is to his lasting glory that he never pretended – to be free."[46]

Undoubtedly, to Victorian readers, the Quran presented itself as something of an anomaly. On the one hand, they did realize its uniqueness, nothing resembling it being known from any other religious tradition. On the other hand, they proceeded on the assumption of its derivativeness, and in the belief that parallels to

---

42 Taylor, *The History of Mohammedanism*, pp. 162–3.
43 *Ibid.*, p. 163.
44 See Maurice, *The Religions of the World*, p. 16.
45 *The Eclectic Magazine*, 1858, p. 468.
46 Smith, *Mohammed and Mohammedanism*, p. 15; see also Stephens, *Christianity and Islam*, pp. 84–5.

numerous elements of it were to be found elsewhere, particularly in Jewish and Christian sources. Those most sympathetic to the Prophet, while aware of the latter, stressed the former, and presented Muhammad as an original religious thinker, or at least as a creative religious reformer. Those least sympathetic to Muhammad made much of the parallels in the Quran to other religious traditions in order at best to denigrate his originality, at worst to shore up their image of the Prophet as imposter.

But for many eighteenth and nineteenth century writers, it was not only the supposed lack of originality of the contents of the Quran which made appreciation of it difficult. It was also a question of its form and style. To the English reader, for whom the paradigm of sacred writings was the Bible, and more specifically its King James version, an empathetic response to the Quran was conceptually and aesthetically unlikely.

Moreover, an English appreciation of the Quran was not helped by the translations in major use during the eighteenth and nineteenth centuries. The French version of du Ryer was itself reasonably faithful to the sense of the original, and the English translation of this, according to Samuel Chew, followed this closely. But Chew argues there was nevertheless a vulgarizing of the spirit and style of the Quran. He sees this as, in part, a lack of literary tact and skill, in part the result of congenital racial and religious antipathy:

> The strange perversions of biblical stories and characters
> irritated Christian readers, who ascribed to deliberate
> malice and calculated blasphemy what was due to
> misunderstanding or ignorance. The soaring eloquence
> which moves Arabs to tears or to shouts of
> joy become in French, and still more in English,
> tasteless extravagance and bombast; the passages
> of homely wisdom and good counsel seem
> merely tedious platitudes, especially
> when this pedestrian version is set in
> contrast to the majestic language of the
> Authorized Version of the Bible; the figurative
> style... required for the transmission of
> something of its beauty a literary art
> beyond the reach of Le Sieur du
> Ryer and his English translator...[47]

This is not merely a case of being wise after the event. For some nineteenth century

---

47 Chew, *The Crescent and the Rose*, p. 451.

writers were aware of the difficulties in translating the Quran, and of the problem with the European versions. In 1826, for example, T. Perronet Thompson criticized Marracci's 1698 *Alcorani textus universus* with its Latin translation. Marracci, according to Thompson, never lost an opportunity of perverting its meaning, or corrupting its simplicity. "If a translation of the Hebrew scriptures," he wrote, "were published, in which every word capable of the change was altered from the reserved and decent one to that which was vulgar and immodest, – and where a licentious commentary was attached to every passage where the subject could, by any perversion, be made the vehicle – attended with insupportable mistranslations and misconstructions for the sake of hanging an odious meaning upon the writer, – it would give some idea of the medium through which the Korān was introduced to Europe."[48]

Without doubt, George Sale's translation of the Quran in 1734 was superior to the English translation of du Ryer, not merely by virtue of the fact that Sale was translating from the Arabic, but also by virtue of his more elegant English. And it supplanted the earlier English version. As Arthur Arberry writes, "this *was* the Koran for all English readers almost to the end of the nineteenth century; many even now living have never looked into any other version."[49] But Sale's work too was not without its critics. The *National Review*, for instance, in its very sympathetic account of the Prophet in 1858, found that "Its rhythm, if not its poetry, is completely destroyed by such a version as that of Sale."[50] And Stanley Lane-Poole in 1883 found Sale's translation insufferably dull, difficult to read and impossible to understand: "On Sale's well-meaning but prosaic work," he concluded, "must be laid much of the responsibility for the prevailing distaste for the Korān."[51]

Even so, with questions of the appropriateness of translations aside, many found its form and style difficult to admire. To be sure, there was a recognition that Muslims saw the Quran as the epitome of Arabic literature in both its style and composition, and some awareness that it was a work to be valued as much in the hearing as in the reading of it. But Gibbon's comments, with Sale and Marracci in front of him, were not untypical: "The harmony and copiousness of style will not reach, in a version, the European infidel: he will peruse with impatience the endless incoherent rhapsody of fable, and precept, and declamation, which seldom excites a sentiment or an idea, which sometimes crawls in the dust, and is sometimes lost in the clouds. The divine attributes exalt the fancy of the Arabian missionary; but his loftiest strains must yield to the sublime simplicity of the book of Job, composed in

---

48 Thompson, "Arabs and Persians," p. 219.
49 Arberry, *The Koran Interpreted*, i. 11.
50 *National Review*, 1858, p. 157.
51 Lane-Poole, *Studies*, p. 116; see also Grant, *The Religions of the World*, p. 32.

a remote age, in the same country and in the same language."⁵² Gibbon admitted that the Quran might appeal more to the devout Arabian. John Roebuck in his *Life of Mahomet* in 1833 was more sceptical. Although he admitted that the language of the Quran might probably possess beauties that only an Arabian could feel, he declared style of no importance in a book of laws, and thought it more than probable "that fashion makes an Arabian pretend to feel beauties which, in reality, he never discovered."⁵³

Opinions remained very much divided throughout the nineteenth century. The *Encyclopaedia Metropolitana* in 1845 declared that "All competent opinions are agreed that the style and diction of the volume in the original, though with many irregularities, are magnificent, harmonious and elegant."⁵⁴ On the other hand, *The Edinburgh Encyclopaedia* in 1830 saw it as a motley collection of incoherent and contradictory fragments.⁵⁵ Such a division of opinion may well have reflected differing judgements on the value of Oriental literture in general. Macaulay's famous minute of 1835 on Indian education reflected one side of this division: "I have read translations of the most celebrated Arabic and Sanskrit works. I have conversed, both here and at home, with men distinguished by their proficiency in the Eastern tongues. I am quite ready to take the oriental learning at the valuation of the orientalists themselves. I have never found one among them who could deny that a single shelf of a good European library was worth the whole native literature of India and Arabia."⁵⁶ But even among those who valued Oriental literature in general, the Quran appeared unrepresentative. *The Foreign Quarterly Review* in 1840, for example, wondered why, in an age when most popular tales and poetry were from the East, the Quran was neglected. Its answer? – because all the most attentive reader can discover is "A tissue of reiterated rhapsody – allusions which are unknown – regulations the necessity and the object of which are not understood – couched too in an idiom and phraseology very different from those of any other work with which he may be acquainted..."⁵⁷ Even Carlyle was hard put to admire it. He found Sale's translation of it "A wearisome confused jumble, crude, incondite; endless iterations, long-windedness, entanglement; most crude, incondite; insupportable stupidity, in short! ... Yet with every allowance, one feels it difficult to see how any mortal ever could consider this Koran as a Book written in Heaven, too good for the Earth; as a well-written book, or indeed as a *book* at all;

52 Gibbon, *Decline and Fall*, iii. 139; see also Mills, *An History*, p. 279 who drew his material from Gibbon without citing his source.
53 Roebuck, *Life of Mahomet*, p. 28.
54 *Encyclopaedia Metropolitana*, 1845, xi. 353.
55 See *The Edinburgh Encyclopaedia*, 1830, xiii. 1.282.
56 Quoted by Said, *The World, The Text, and the Critic*, p. 12.
57 *The Foreign Quarterly Review*, 1840, p. 1.

and not a bewildered rhapsody; *written*, so far as writing goes, as badly as almost any book ever was."⁵⁸ Yet Carlyle, in spite of all this, *was* able to empathise with the Muslim love of the Quran as a book from the heart able to reach all hearts; and he did find in its rhapsodical chaos the confused ferment of a great, rude, human soul "struggling vehemently to utter itself in words."⁵⁹

Unassimilable to Western tastes it may have been, but others, like Carlyle, recognised its literary power. George Sale was fully aware that his translation did not come up to the original. And he recognized that its form and style in Arabic could not be imitated. Still, for Sale, "The style of the Korān is generally beautiful and fluent, especially where it imitates the prophetic manner and Scripture phrases. It is concise, and often obscure, adorned with bold figures after the eastern taste, enlivened with florid and sententious expressions, and in many places, especially where the majesty and attributes of God are described, sublime and magnificent."⁶⁰ William Muir, a century and a quarter later, although finding the later parts of the Quran artifical nevertheless saw its style as reflecting the wild exuberance of the Prophet:

> At first, like a mountain stream, the current dashes
> headlong, pure, wild, impetuous. Advancing, the
> language becomes calmer and more uniform, yet
> ever and anon, mingled with oaths and wild
> ejaculations, we come upon a tumultuous rhapsody,
> like the unexpected cataract, charged with thrilling
> words of conviction and fervid aspiration. Onward
> still, though the dancing stream sometimes sparkles
> and foam deceives the eye, we trace a rapid decline in the
> vivid energy of natural inspiration, and
> even the mingling with it of earth-born
> elements.⁶¹

Judgements of the Quran during the nineteenth century were so varied that it is difficult to find any coherent pattern. Surprisingly, in contrast to the seventeenth and eighteenth century discussions of the work, there is even less detailed analysis of its contents. Discussion of it, particularly among those unsympathetic to Muhammad, tended to be limited to the mere recitation of a fairly standardised

---

58 Carlyle, *On Heroes*, pp. 64–5.
59 *Ibid.*, p. 66.
60 Sale, *The Koran*, p. 47.
61 Muir, *The Life of Moḥammad*, p. 70; see also Lane-Poole, *Studies*, pp. 167–8; Badger, "Mohammed," p. 95; Palmer, *The Qur'ān*, p. lxxvii; *The Dublin Review*, 1878, p. 405.

litany of errors. The pattern was perhaps set in the first English translation: contradictions, blasphemies, obscene speeches, ridiculous fables, rude and incongruous – this was the core of its contents.[62] Porteus in 1800 found it dull, heavy and monotonous, with trivial, disgusting, and even immoral precepts.[63] The *Encyclopaedia Britannica* in 1842 declared it incoherent, repetitive, and vague, with contradictions and absurdities almost without number.[64] And George Badger in 1875 criticized Bosworth Smith for failing to be specific about the numerous fables, discrepancies, contradictions, anachronisms, and distortions to be met with in the Quran.[65]

The little detailed analysis of its contents may be attributed to the fact that the focus of nineteenth century discussions of Islam was not the Quran but Muhammad himself. The book took second place to analysis of the life and character of the man; and judgements of the former were based on prior decisions about the latter. Carlyle was one of the few who valued the man but viewed the book critically. But even he read it, as we have seen, as the record of a human hero. And those who saw Muhammad, not as an imposter, but rather as a man of courage, integrity, and sincerity, took a quite different view of it. John Moehler in 1847, for instance, found an original piety and a touching devotion within it; and he maintained that it nourished an estimable religious and moral life.[66] Washington Irving saw those parts of the Quran that derived from the Meccan period as pure and elevated, breathing a poetical if not religious inspiration.[67] *Harper's New Monthly Magazine* in 1877 read the Quran as the work of an active and eager intellect struggling against the mores of his time to attain humanity and to aid progress.[68] In 1903, that sympathiser with Carlyle, W. Quartermaine East, fervently concluded his account of the Quran,

> Such was the flow of thoughts emanating from
> an Arab, fervently praying the unknown to
> deliver his tribe from the unseen terrors of
> idolatry, – thoughts converted into words, and
> soaring into sublimity, all based upon principles
> as old as the world's foundations, leaving for the

---

62 See du Ryer, *The Alcoran*, Preface; see also Herbert, *Some Years Travels*, p. 338.
63 See Porteus, *A Summary*, p. 81.
64 *The Encyclopaedia Britannica*, 1842, xiv. 32.
65 See Badger, "Mohammed," p. 95.
66 See Moehler, *On the Relation of Islam*, p. 23; see also *The Encyclopaedia Britannica*, 1853–60, xv. 303.
67 See Irving, *Life of Mahomet*, p. 236.
68 *Harper's*, 1877, p. 411; see also Blyden, *Christianity*, pp. 6–7.

> faithful a code of noble universality as wide in conception, as world-wide in its destinies, embracing the truth of Confucius, the justice of Plato, the self-abnegation of Buddha, and the all-comprising love of the world's great teacher.[69]

Despite the awareness that it was the Quran itself that was the primary focus of Islamic piety, and despite the realization that the role of Muhammad in Islam was not analogous to that of Christ in Christianity, the continuing use of the term "Mohammedanism" or similar alternatives during the nineteenth century, among both admirers and detractors, is a potent symbol of the inability of Western writers to construe Islam in a way not in accord with paradigm of Christianity. To be sure, the Quran was utilized to reinforce positive assessments of the Prophet. But it was the nature and character of Muhammad that remained significantly of more importance than the text of the Quran within the nineteenth century context. As Carlyle put it, "Great men are the inspired (speaking and acting) texts of that divine *Book of Revelation*, whereof a Chapter is completed from epoch to epoch, and by some named *History*."[70] And consequently, I think it true to say that, during the nineteenth century, although there was a drift towards more positive assessments of the Quran, it failed to keep pace with the quite significant shifts in attitudes to the Prophet during the same period.

3. The Religion of the Book

But if attitudes to the Quran remained varied while attitudes to the Prophet significantly changed, it was the success of Muhammad and Islam that most cried out for explanation. Of all the questions about Islam, this had impinged most painfully on the Christian tradition, and on the West in general. During the eighteenth and nineteenth centuries, there were two main ways of explaining the success of Islam. The first was to show it as part of a continuing divine dispensation, as merely a continuation of the Christian God's providential action in the world. The second, often appearing side by side with the former, was to construe its success solely as the result of natural factors.

In fact, a variety of reasons were given to illumine Islam's success as part of the

---

69 East, *The Last Days of Great Men*, p. 279.
70 Quoted by Houghton, *The Victorian Frame of Mind*, p. 314.

divine providence. It was maintained, for example, that God was testing his people in order to keep them in awe and obedience, or that he wanted to bring about a union of Christian princes, and to punish Greek emperors, heretics, and schismatics.[71] Boulainvilliers in 1731 saw Islam utilized by God to confound the Christians of the East, to overthrow the empires of the Greeks and Romans, and to subjugate the Persians: "In short, to spread the knowledge of the Unity of GOD from *India* to *Spain*; and to suppress every other worship besides his own."[72]

Islam the "natural religion" and divine scourge of idolatry was one image. Islam as a general instrument of God's wrath for human wickedness was another.[73] To the anonymous author of a life of Muhammad in 1851, God allowed Islam to succeed "in order to make known his indignation against the degenerate Christians of those days, and to intimate to the church of future times the danger of neglecting the word of God."[74] Even as late as 1895, Grant could recognize the success of Islam as a rebuke to Christendom.[75]

But throughout the eighteenth and nineteenth centuries, naturalistic factors were more often invoked to explain Islam's phenomenal success. In part, this was a continuation of traditional Christian explanations of Islam's fortunes. For Christian apologists, the success of Christianity was evidence of its divine attestation; and naturalistic explanations of Islam's success were thus intended to deny the possibility of its being divinely favoured, leaving the success of Christianity only as inexplicable apart from God. But the development of secular history also, especially in the nineteenth century guaranteed the predominance of naturalistic explanations of Islam, even if, at the same time, it made unfeasible theological interpretations of the success of Christianity.[76]

A large variety of natural factors were put up. One popular and effective argument was the Muslim use of force. It generally occurred high in the catalogues of reasons for Islam's success. As one writer put it in 1847, "But for the victories of his sword, there is no reason to believe that he would ever have been heard of beyond his own country."[77] And it provided, as we saw in Chapter Two, a useful counterpoint to Christianity's self-image of its own success as the result of peaceful persuasion and divine blessing.

71 See e.g., Ross, *Pansebeia*, pp. 178–9.
72 Boulainvilliers, *The Life of Mahomet*, p. 166.
73 See e.g., anon., *The Life of Mahomet*, 1799, pp. 169–70.
74 Anon., *Life of Mohammad*, 1851, p. 25; see also p. 112.
75 Grant, *The Religions of the World*, p. 37.
76 It was Forster's belief that naturalistic explantions of Islam's success were the thin end of the wedge leading to similar accounts of Christianity, that motivated his providential view of both religions. See Forster, *Mahometanism Unveiled*, Introduction, and i. 66, 69.
77 Anon., *The Life of Mohammed*, 1847, p. 155.

Muhammad's opportunism was another common explanation. The prophet pandered to common tastes, adapted rites to pre-conceived opinions, and appealed to the prejudices and passions of those he addressed.[78] According to Charles Mills, the appeal of a fanatic, particularly among Asiatics, was a crucial factor.[79] For many, it was the attitude to sensual indulgence in Islam that attracted corruptly-inclined Easterners, together with its promise of a sensual Paradise.[80] The strictness of the Islamic moral code, or the commitment of its adherents to the injunctions of the Quran, were generally ignored. The claim of George Miller in 1816 that the true solution to the question of the success of Islam lay in the intrinsic merits of its doctrines[81] was a rare exception to the general rule that its success was best explained by what were seen as the moral defects of its teachings, or its founder.

The success of Islam was often also ascribed to the evil, ignorance, and superstition of the Arabs of Muhammad's time. Joseph White was typical of eighteenth century opinions. To him, nothing contributed more effectively to the success of Islam than "the extreme and deplorable want of all intellectual culture, under which the far greater part of the Arabians then laboured."[82] The picture painted of pre-Islamic society was often a gloomy one, though lightened in many nineteenth century writings by the image of the noble Arab. To *The Quarterly Review* in 1877, for example, the Arab was a free, simple, and vigorous child of nature. But there was a darker side: "Morally and intellectually, they were in a state of revolting barbarism; the primitive simplicity of Sabaeanism... had degenerated into a gloomy and idolatrous polytheism; drunkenness, gambling, divination by arrows, polygamy, murder, and worse vices were terribly rife amongst them."[83]

Such an argument was something of a two-edged sword. On the one hand, it implied that the success of Islam was the result of ignorance and evil, and on the other, that Islam, at least to some extent had improved the moral and religious qualities of its adherents. But further, it raised the question why Islam had been able to succeed in Arabia where Christianity hadn't. For many then, there was a clear need (particularly in the light of the fact that Islam, in Arabia at the time of Muhammad and elsewhere later, had supplanted Christianity) to answer the Muslim claim that Islam was the final, superior, comprehensive, definitive revelation.

---

78 See e.g., White, *Sermons*, p. 53; Porteus, *A Summary*, p. 62; Ross, *Pansebeia*, pp. 175–7; anon., *The Life of Mahomet*, 1799, p. 168.
79 See Mills, *A History*, pp. 170–1.
80 See e.g., White, *Sermons*, p. 45; but cf. *The Encyclopaedia Britannica*, 1853–60, xv. 302.
81 See Miller, *Lectures*, i. 235–7; see also Palmer, *The Qur'ān*, p. xlix–l.
82 White, *Sermons*, p. 42; see also Taylor, *The History of Mohammedanism*, p. 67; Freeman, *History and Conquest of the Saracens*, pp. 27–8; Palmer, *The Qur'ān*, p. x.
83 *The Quarterly Review*, 1877, p. 214.

The answer, universally endorsed, was a simple one: The Christianity supplanted by Islam was not true Christianity. The image of a Christianity divided by heresy, and factionalism, and permeated by impiety, inequity, iniquity, and idolatry was a feature of most accounts of Islam in the eighteenth and nineteenth centuries. Here, Stubbe and Boulanvilliers concurred with Joseph White,[84] Godfrey Higgins and Bosworth Smith with William Sime and The Religious Tract Society.[85] Having depicted the state of Arabia and the Christianity within it in such dark colours, many affected – sometimes disingenuously, but often sincerely – to be little surprised at the success of Islam.

And there was a sense in which eighteenth and nineteenth century Protestantism, in its simplicity, both ritually and doctrinally, in its commitment to the Bible, in its antipathy to the perceived idolatries of both Western Catholicism and Eastern Orthodoxy, did have a formal similarity to Islam. Protestants could empathise with the success of Islam over such forms of Christianity. As one anonymous author put it as early as 1735, Islam "is to me nearer to the true Christian System, than what was believed or practised among those who in his [Muhammad's] Days blasphemously called themselves Christians; or than is professed by Papists, especially, at this day, or any other Sect of Christians without the Pale of the Protestant Church..."[86] Over a century later, Henry Milman admitted that it would have been astounding if thousands, weary of interminable Christian controversies, had not sought refuge in Muhammad's simple, intelligible truth of the Divine Unity.[87]

4. Islam and Culture

There were numerous works on Islam, then, that viewed it as bringing about a significant improvement on the intellectual, moral, and religious climate of pre-Islamic Arabia. But many of these also saw Islam as having either degenerated after Muhammad, or as incapable of change after his time. Even among those works sympathetic to Muhammad and to the Islam of his time, there was little enthusiasm for later developments of it. A discourse of Islam as static, stagnant, and unchan-

---

84 See Stubbe, *An Account*, p. 72; Boulainvilliers, *The Life of Mahomet*, p. 217; White, *Sermons*, p. 33.
85 See Higgins, *An Apology*, p. 1; Smith, *Mohammed and Mohammedanism*, p. 135; Sime, *History of Mohammed*, pp. 11–12; anon.; *The Life of Mohammed*, 1847, pp. 30–1.
86 Anon., *Reflections on Mohammedism*, 1735, p. 28.
87 See Milman, *History*, ii. 46–7.

ging, or of modern Islam as decadent and degenerate permeated many texts. William Cooke Taylor, for example, was an admirer of Muhammad, but he saw the spirit and vitality of Islam as having departed forever: "every disease," he argued, "became permanent in its system, every wound changed into a festering sore, until at length it is little better than the warlike carcase..."[88] While the *British Quarterly Review* for 1872 saw Muhammad as one of the great reformers, when his system went beyond Arabia, it declared, "it became the greatest of curses to mankind."[89] As Bryan Turner aptly puts it, "The rise of Islam is thus the genesis of its demise."[90]

The inability of Victorians, however much they admired Muhammad and original Islam, to endorse its contemporary manifestations, arose from a deep-seated incapacity of nineteenth century England to treat Islam, indeed the East in general, on equal terms. The West tended only to be able to deal with it from the assumption of its own essential and unquestionable superiority. Indeed, the greater value of the West over the East, over all those it variously characterized as backward, degenerate, or uncivilized was a *sine qua non* of most discussions of non-Western forms of life. And the rigid sense of fundamental differences between East and West, Orient and Occident, permeated most nineteenth century studies not only of Islam, but of Buddhism, Hinduism, and the so-called primitive religions.

Seldom far beneath the surface was the image of the progressive West over against a static or degenerate East. According to Kathryn Tidrick, during the nineteenth century, "The 'unchanging East' came to be regarded as a spectacle; one for which, it was increasingly assumed, the English were entitled to both a front seat and a presence behind the scenes."[91] And the image of a vibrant, active, progressive Christianity over against a passive, inert Islam was congenial to a policy of British political and religious hegemony. The demise of Islam seemed certain: "the discoveries of science are against it. The improvements in government are against it. Above all, the truth of the Christian religion is against it... *here are elements of power which neither the religion nor the empire of Mohammed can finally resist.*" [92]

It remained a common motif through the nineteenth century. Edward Freeman for example saw Muhammad as an instrument in the hands of God and original Islam as crucial to Eastern reform. But he nonetheless defined the West as progressive, legal, monogamous, and Christian, and the East as arbitrary, stationary,

---

88 Taylor, *The History of Mohammedanism*, p. 5.
89 *British Quarterly Review*, 1872, p. 132; see also Badger, "Mohammed," pp. 96, 98.
90 Turner, "Orientalism," p. 373.
91 Tidrick, *Heart-beguiling Araby*, p. 50.
92 Anon., *Life of Mohammad*, 1851, p. 173 (my italics).

polygamous, and Mahometan.[93] To William Muir, Islam may have been quite suitable to Arabia thirteen centuries before, but was quite unsuited to other times and places: "it binds society hand and foot."[94] In contrast, he maintained, Christianity was capable of adaptation to all ages, its doctrines harmonising with every upward step towards freedom, knowledge, and philanthropy. Christianity was compatible with progress, Islam was not. "In short," Muir concluded, "the distinction between the two creeds is, that while the aspirations of humanity have free play under the Gospel, in the swathing bands of the Coran they are altogether checked and stifled."[95]

Thus, Islam was often seen as the source of all the evils which, in the Western imagination at least, afflicted Islamic societies. It was Islam, extravagant but not progressive, that had relieved the Eastern mind from the discipline of improving itself, and had left it in its preferred state of untamed wilderness.[96] To T. C. Trowbridge in 1882, Islam was the prime source of the political decrepitude, and the moral and social evils of the Ottoman Turks.[97] Ernst Renan was of the opinion that Islam and modern European culture were not incompatible.[98] But his was an isolated voice. More would have inclined towards the Baptist George Smith's opinion. To him it was certain that "Islam and scientific and political progress are incompatible, as Christianity and scientific and political progress are not incompatible."[99]

There was a number of aspects of Islam which were often cited as the cause of the stagnation and decadence of Islamic societies. Some saw it in blind devotion to Muhammad[100]; others in the dead weight of Islamic fatalism.[101] William Palgrave, somewhat obtusely, saw the doctrine of Divine omnipotence as having hindered scientific development "by reducing every phenomenon at once to the one immediate universal and arbitrary cause,"[102] without making it clear why the analogous Christian doctrine would not have had the same effect. And, somewhat extraordinarily, he viewed the Muslim ban on alcohol as a major cause in Islam's inability to progress, and to be tolerant.[103] The *Dublin University Magazine* for 1873 blamed

---

93 See Freeman, *History and Conquest of the Saracens*, p. 4.
94 Muir, "Islam and Christianity," p. 134.
95 *Ibid.*, p. 134.
96 See *The Christian Remembrancer*, 1846, p. 437.
97 See Trowbridge, "Mohammedanism," p. 289.
98 See Renan, *Studies*, pp. 210–11; but cf. Grant, *Religions of the World*, p. 40.
99 Smith, *Mohammedanism*, p. 26; see also Gairdner, *The Reproach of Islam*, p. 182.
100 See e.g., Trowbridge, "Mohammedanism," p. 289; Johnstone, *Muhammad and his Power*, p. 159.
101 See Gairdner, *The Reproach of Islam*, pp. 136–7.
102 Palgrave, *Narrative*, i. 433.
103 *Ibid.*, i. 148.

the Islamic doctrine of God for the social evils of Islamic countries: "Christianity says 'God is love'; Mohammedanism says, 'God is will.' Christianity says 'Trust in God;' Mohammedanism says, 'Submit to God.' Hence the hardness, coldness and cruelty of the system; hence its utter inability to establish any good government."[104] The Jesuit E. Power put it succinctly in 1909. God, he said, is not a father, but a master, "like an Eastern despot distributing arbitrarily rewards and punishments."[105]

Islam was seen too as reinforcing the tendency of Eastern cultures to remain static and unchanging. To *The North British Review* in 1855, it had finally rendered the stationary Asiatic even more stationary than before.[106] Robert Osborn's *Islam under the Arabs* was much criticized by Edward Blyden for endorsing a medieval image of Islam, and therefore for being out of touch with the more enlightened and tolerant view of Islam prevalent among Victorian writers.[107] And overall, Blyden was correct. But Osborn's view, certainly more flamboyantly expressed than was common, that Islam and progress were incompatible was not unusual: "Chained to a black stone in a barren wilderness, the heart and reason of the Muhammadan world would seem to have taken the similitude of the objects they reverence; and the refreshing dews and genial sunshine which fertilise all else seek in vain for anything to quicken there."[108]

Intimately connected with the static nature of Muslim societies, in the view of many, was Oriental despotism, and the servitude of the multitudes that resulted from it. In spite of the innate penchant of Asiatics for despotism, explained Johannes Döllinger in 1838, Islam had undoubtedly developed it.[109] What other religion, asked Gairdner seventy years later, "has so uniformly tended to produce, and to acquiesce in tyrants, with their inevitable following of toadies, cringers, and abjects, as this power-worshipping faith?"[110]

The perceived relationship between Islam and despotism was further reinforced by an inclination to see the Turks as paradigmatic Muslims. And Victorian writers saw Turkey as most fully exemplifying the worst features of Islamic societies. To George Miller in 1816, the Arabs had improved and refined Islam, but the Turks

---

104 *Dublin University Magazine*, 1873, p. 476.
105 Power, *The Religion of the Korān*, p. 31.
106 See *The North British Review*, 1855, p. 459; see also *Dublin University Magazine*, 1873, p. 477.
107 See Blyden, *Christianity*, pp. 248–50.
108 Osborn, *Islam*, p. 84.
109 See Döllinger, *Muhammad's Religion*, p. 38.
110 Gairdner, *The Reproach of Islam*, p. 139.

remained barbarians.¹¹¹ In contrast, *The National Quarterly Review* for 1876 was sympathetic neither to the Turks nor Islam. In the Turks of the present day, it declared, "maintaining with difficulty an empire tottering to its fall, indolent, self-indulgent and vicious, yet bigoted and cruel... we may perceive the legitimate results of the principles and religion of Mohammed."¹¹²

Not surprisingly there were some attempts to defend Islam in principle from the alleged defects of its adherents. Bosworth Smith, for example, suggested quite reasonably that a religion ought not to be judged by its perversions and corruptions. It was as unfair, he maintained, to judge Islam in terms of Turkish despots, maniac dervishes, and Persian libertines, as to judge Christianity in terms of Anabaptists, Pillar Saints, or Shakers.¹¹³ But there did remain a tendency throughout the Victorian period to blame Islam for all the imagined ills of Oriental societies – the moral degradation of women, slavery, the physical and mental debilities of men, envy, violence and cruelty, the disquiet and misery of private life, the continual agitations, commotions, and revolutions of public life. As the *Dublin University Magazine* for 1873 summed it up, "It is a hard, cold, cruel, empty faith, which should give way to the purer forms of a higher civilisation."¹¹⁴

But if judgements on contemporary Islam were overwhelmingly negative, there was much more variation in opinions on the truth and value of original Islam. To be sure negative assessments were present, though seldom did they equal the vituperativeness of the medieval or early modern periods.¹¹⁵ In particular, it was the externals of Islam that were often singled out for criticism. John Roebuck in 1833, for example, highlighted the idle, ridiculous, useless, and sometimes mischievous observances. These were sufficient evidence for him of the low character of Muhammad's religion and morality.¹¹⁶ Undoubtedly, the rise of Evangelicalism played some role in criticisms of this sort. The Evangelical stress on inner piety and moral seriousness underlaid much of the discourse. Thus, for instance, the *Home and Foreign Review* for 1864 concluded,

> A short and uniformly monotonous form of prayer;
> a few external ceremonies, almost all intimately

---

111 See Miller, *Lectures*, i. 224–5; but cf. the critical review in *The Edinburgh Review*, 1829–30, pp. 312–3, 323–4.
112 *The National Quarterly Review*, 1876, p. 228; see also pp. 226–7.
113 See Smith, *Mohammed and Mohammedanism*, p. 265; see also *The Eclectic Magazine*, 1862, pp. 214–5.
114 *The Dublin University Magazine*, 1873, p. 480; see also *The Encyclopaedia Britannica*, 1842, xiv. 39.
115 See e. g., Smith, *Gods Arrovve*, ch. 4; *Travailes*, p. 47; Smith, *Remarks*, p. 27; Tillotson, *The Works*, p. 182.
116 See Roebuck, *Life of Mahomet*, p. 29.

connected with whatever is most animal, most
debasing in human nature; a most servile fear of a
most material hell; a most base desire of a heaven of wine
and harlots; a blind and inexorable destiny for God; and
a crowd of slaves for creatures or worshipers; – such
is Islam.[117]

Stanley Lane-Poole was, as we have seen, well-disposed towards Islam. He praised Islam for its simple, austere theism, its lofty conception of the relation of humanity to God, and its noble doctrine of the duty of man to man. But he too saw it as over-formal and rigid, leaving too little to the believer, and too much to ritual.[118] George Badger, not so well-disposed, agreed: "the best that can be said of it is, that it inculcates external rectitude only, with the adjunct of mechanical devotions, the outward performance of which is all that is insisted on."[119]

For a few, Islam both in theory and practice remained the religion of the Imposter, the implacable foe of Christianity, and the work of Satan.[120] But there were some who wanted to argue that Islam had had, in some places, a civilizing influence. Apologists for Islam made much of its benevolent influence in Africa.[121] As Bosworth Smith put it, "if the question must be put, whether it is the Mohammedan or Christian nations that have as yet done most for Africa, the answer must be that it is not the Christian. And if it be asked, again, not what religion is the purest in itself, and ideally the best... but which... is the religion most likely to get hold on a vast scale of the native mind, and so in some measure to elevate the savage character, the same answer must be returned."[122]

Others remained unconvinced by such apologies. The *Quarterly Review* for 1877 suggested that even if Islam had raised African tribes from the depths of ignorance, superstition, brutality, and vice, this did not entail that the religion itself was an unmixed good, and capable of universal application.[123] Still others bemoan-

---

117 *Home and Foreign Review*, 1864, p. 557.
118 See Lane-Poole, *Studies*, p. 99.
119 Badger, "Mohammed," p. 91.
120 See e.g., Freeman, *History and Conquest of the Saracens*, pp. 70–3; van Mildert, *Infidelity*, i. 227; Koelle, *Mohammed and Mohammedanism*, p. 471.
121 See especially Daniel, *Islam, Europe and Empire*, ch. 11.
122 Smith, *Mohammed and Mohammedanism*, p. 47; see also Blyden, *Christianity*; Reade, *The Martyrdom of Man*, pp. 280–2; Blunt, *The Future of Islam*, pp. 25–7, 172–3; Moehler, *On the Relation of Islam*, p. 40; Smith, *Mohammedanism*, pp. 16–17; Lane-Poole, *Studies*, pp. 113–4.
123 See *The Quarterly Review*, 1877, p. 234.

ed the fact that the hold of Islam in Africa, irrespective of the benefits it conferred, made the task of Christian evangelism all that much harder.[124]

But there was a general consensus that, as Islam had improved the lot of the Arabians at the time of the Prophet, so also it had been of benefit to other so-called savage cultures. Most writers on Islam saw it as more entitled to praise than other non-Christian religions. Even Charles Forster found its merits "confessedly superior to those of every other religious system which has obtained amongst men;"[125] and he saw it as a stepping stone from Heathenism to Christianity, from idolatry to the eventual universal diffusion of the Gospel. Forster's view, to be sure, was based not so much on a sympathetic view of Islam as on his apocalyptic view of Christian history. And it was this that the Edinburgh reviewer found objectionable. "It is to the faith of Mr. Forster," he declared, "and not his charity, that we owe his ambiguous patronage of this new Christian heresy."[126] And he went on to comment wryly, that if Forster was right, missionary societies should devote themselves to the printing of cheap Qurans, and the sending of "missionary Moolahs" to the heathen.[127] On the other side of the Christian divide from Forster, John Henry Newman argued that no Catholic need deny that Islam was a great improvement on paganism. Muhammad, he maintained, taught much of truth and importance: "He stands in his creed between the religion of God and the religion of devils, between Christianity and idolatry, between the West and the extreme East."[128] Barthélemy Saint-Hilaire in 1865 went as far as to declare that, with the exception of Christianity, no other religion could compare with it.[129] But it was Bosworth Smith who, perhaps more than any other, signalled the shift in general attitudes to non-Christian religions during the Victorian period which made possible altered images of Muhammad and Islam. The comparative study of religion, he argued, is beginning to teach,

> not indeed that all religions are equally true or equally elevating, but that all contain some truth; that no religion is exclusively good, none exclusively bad; that any religion which has a real and continued hold on a large body of mankind must

---

124 See e.g., Muir, *The Life of Mohammad*, p. 523; Gairdner, *The Reproach of Islam*, pp. 210–11; *The North British Review*, 1855, p. 457; *British Quarterly Review*, 1872, p. 134.
125 Forster, *Mahometanism Unveiled*, i. 103–4.
126 *The Edinburgh Review*, 1829–30, p. 329.
127 *Ibid.*, p. 331.
128 Newman, *Lectures*, p. 106.
129 See Barthélemy Saint-Hilaire, *Mahomet et le Coran*, p. x.

satisfy a real spiritual need, and is so far good.[130]

Although he was committed to the superiority of Christianity, as were all nineteenth century comparative religionists, his acceptance of principles such as these enabled him to conclude that Islam was the nearest approach to Christianity, and that Muhammad was truly a Prophet: "Mohammed to the end of his life claimed for himself that title only with which he had begun, and which the highest philosophy and the truest Christianity will one day, I venture to believe, agree in yielding to him – that of a Prophet, a very Prophet of God."[131]

5. The Noble Arab?

Throughout the course of this study, I have suggested that, during the Victorian period, there was a significant shift towards positive assessments of Muhammad. For some he remained a heretic, but for many he was an heroic figure. It remains then to give this further substance by paying more attention than heretofore to the many very general descriptions of his physical attributes and his general demeanour.

Most sixteenth and seventeenth century accounts depicted him in somewhat satanic ways, and were merely the products of a vivid Western imagining. Sebastian Muenster in 1572, for example, spoke of his "straunge and horrible countinance, his terrible voyce, and his desperate ruffenly boldness, greatly to be feared."[132] And George Sandys in 1608 described him as "Mean of stature... and evil-proportioned: having ever a scald head, which (as some say) made him wear a white Shash continually: now worn by his Sectaries."[133]

Such descriptions had disappeared by the beginning of the eighteenth century. Indeed, as was often the case, Henry Stubbe in the 1670's was among the first to use Muslim descriptions of Muhammad's physical features and personality. These descriptions were themselves highly idealized portraits of him who was in the Muslim view, the most beautiful of all humankind. As Annemarie Schimmel writes; for Muslims "Muhammad becomes the archetype of all human beauty."[134] Thus,

130 Smith, *Mohammed and Mohammedanism*, p. 249.
131 *Ibid.*, p. 291; see also *The Quarterly Review*, 1877, p. 237; *The Dublin Review*, 1878, p. 424.
132 Muenster, *Cosmographye*, p. 62.
133 Sandys, *Travailes*, p. 42; see also Heylyn, *Cosmographie*, p. 121.
134 Schimmel, *Muhammad*, p. 35.

from the eighteenth century onwards, the physical description of Muhammad given in the West is that of the *beau ideal* of Arab manhood.

An anonymous Life in 1712 pictured him as of a proper and middle stature, comely, fair and ruddy, with a large head, a long neck and aquiline nose, black piercing eyes, a large mouth and a sweet voice; a man who delighted in sweet smells, of ready wit, undaunted courage, courteous, and charitable.[135] Of particular importance was the description of Muhammad given by Abu'l-Fida in the *De Vita et rebus gestis Mohammedis* of Gagnier in 1723, for its description often was repeated in the next one hundred and fifty years. According to this, Muhammad was of middle stature, handsome, with a broad chest, a powerful neck, large hands and feet; he had a large head, long black hair, flashing black eyes, fine and long eyebrows with a prominent vein between which swelled when he was angry, and, between his shoulders the "seal of prophethood" – a mole the size of a pidgeon's egg. He was quiet, affable, temperate, abstemious, with a passion for ointments and perfumes, and exhilarated by women.[136] Abu'l-Fida's Life, as we have noted earlier, was a late one, but his description of the Prophet did closely parallel that of the oldest descriptions.[137]

Such characteristics, and others later added to the catalogue from other Muslim sources, became standard in nineteenth century accounts of the Prophet. And they occurred even in works which, in other ways, were highly critical of Muhammad and Islam. Both Carlyle and Washington Irving played a significant role in creating and popularising this picture[138], as did William Muir's catalogue of the features of Muhammad drawn from the biographies of Ibn Sa'd and others.[139] Muir's account was used by Bosworth Smith, and its influence thus extended even further.[140] In effect, virtually every reader of any work on Muhammad during the nineteenth century would have received an almost identical composite image of the Prophet. The description in the *National Review* for 1861 is briefer than most, but not untypical in its picturing of Muhammad both as the ideal noble Arab and the prophetic Hero:

> Tall and spare and of amazing strength with his
> cheek still ruddy, and his beard falling in

---

135 See anon., "The Life and Actions of Mahomet, extracted chiefly from Mahometan Authors," in *Four Treatises*, pp. 78–9.
136 See Gagnier, *Ismael Abu'l-Feda*.
137 See Schimmel, *Muhammad*, p. 34.
138 See Carlyle, *On Heroes*, p. 53; Irving, *Life of Mahomet*, p. 230; see also *Dublin University Magazine*, 1876, p. 137; anon., *Life of Mohammed*, 1851, pp. 112–3.
139 See Muir, *The Life of Moḥammad*, pp. 510–36.
140 See Smith, *Mohammed and Mohammedanism*, pp. 109–12.

> black waves just streaked with silver to
> his waist, his manner soft to feminine grace,
> his eyes black, restless and slightly bloodshot and
> his gait... firm but springing, he must
> have looked as fit to be a leader of
> men as any the Arabs had ever seen.[141]

But those very attributes possessed by Muhammad, which to many were evidence of a nobility of character, were to others merely signs of the enormity of his duplicity. The life of Muhammad appended to the 1757 edition of Ockley's *The History of the Saracens* drew in part on Sale (himself dependent on Abu'l-Fida) for its description but with the opposite intent. The Muslim authors, claimed its probable author Dr Long,

> extol Mohammed as a man of fine parts,
> and a strong memory, of few words, of a cheerful
> aspect, affable and complaisant in his behaviour.
> They also celebrate his justice, clemency,
> generosity, modesty, abstinence, and humility...
> However, to judge of him by his actions
> as related by these same writers, we cannot
> help concluding, that he was a very subtle and
> crafty man, who put on the appearance only of
> those good qualities; while the governing
> principles of his soul were ambition and lust.[142]

In contrast, *The Edinburgh Review* for 1866 presented Muhammad as the very antithesis of its ideal of noble Arab manliness. In the imagination of the Edinburgh reviewer, the ideal Arab was a fiery-souled irresistible warrior, bold in speech, indulging in wine, women, and song, a gambler, not prone to tears, indefatigable in combat with limbs as iron as his armour. But Muhammad was, for this writer, quite the opposite. Muhammad lacked the attributes which made up this ideal and which, more importantly, might be said also to make up the ideal of Victorian manliness (at

---

141 *National Review*, 1861, p. 321; see also *Chamber's Encyclopaedia*, 1874, vi. 501; *Harper's*, 1877, p. 404; Lane-Poole, *Studies*, pp. 37–41; Palmer, *The Qur'ān*, pp. xix–xx; Johnstone, *Muhammad and His Power*, p. 148; East, *The Last Days of Great Men*, pp. 270–1; Margoliouth, *Mohammed*, pp. 63–4; Gairdner, *The Reproach of Islam*, p. 51; Holland, *The Story of Mohammed*, pp. 37–8.
142 Ockley, *The History of the Saracens*, pp. 62–3; see also anon., *The Life of Mohammed*, 1847, pp. 92, 167.

least in its aristocratic rather than bourgeois form). His language was clearly calculated to evoke in the reader an image of an unmanly, feminine Muhammad:

> he had inherited from his mother a delicate,
> nervous, and extremely impressionable
> constitution. He was gifted with an exaggerated
> and sickly sensibility; he had a woman's love
> for fine scents and perfumes; he was melancholy,
> silent, fond of desert places, solitary walks, and
> lonely meditations at set of sun in the valleys; full
> of vague restlessness, weeping and sobbing
> like a child when he was in pain; subject
> to attacks of epilepsy, and without courage
> in the field of battle.[143]

In fact, the reviewer appears to have mined his sources – Caussin de Perceval, Weil, Muir, Sprenger, Barthélemy Saint-Hilaire, and Renan, solely with a view to discrediting the image of Muhammad as a noble Arab, and, one might add, as a gentleman. For him, it was a blasphemy to name him in the same breath as Jesus Christ. He was hardly even capable of comparison with the Buddha, who stood "as much above Mahomet as Mahomet does above the founder of American Mormonism."[144]

For a number of other critics, it was Muhammad *as* the ideal noble Arab who stood in such contrast to Jesus. As an anonymous Life in 1799 somewhat colourfully put it, "Ah, Mahomet, Mahomet, when I see thy sword reeking with the blood of men, and hear Jesus exclaiming upon Calvary, 'father, forgive them for they know not what they do;' I am obliged to conclude that the devil was thy constituent."[145] The same point was made by William Muir sixty years later, albeit less dramatically[146], while *The Dublin Review* in 1878 remarked that, when Muhammad as the founder of a religion is compared with Jesus, "the abyss between the two lives is manifest at the first glance…"[147]

Many remained perplexed by Muhammad's character. William Muir warned his readers against seeking a consistency in Muhammad.[148] Washington Irving too was puzzled by the combination of heartfelt piety and worldly concerns. He found it

---

143 *The Edinburgh Review*, 1866, p. 19.
144 *Ibid.*, p. 49.
145 Anon., *The Life of Mahomet*, 1799, p. 51.
146 See Muir, "Islam and Christianity," p. 134.
147 *The Dublin Review*, 1878, p. 411.
148 See Muir, *The Life of Moḥammad*, pp. 522–3; see also *The Edinburgh Review*, 1866, pp. 48–9; *Harper's*, 1877, p. 411.

difficult to reconcile "such ardent, persevering piety with an incessant system of blasphemous imposture; nor such pure and elevated and benignant precepts as are contained in the Koran, with a mind haunted by ignoble passions, and devoted to the grovelling interests of mere mortality..."[149] *Chamber's Encyclopaedia* in 1874 felt able to conclude that, all in all, the history of humanity has seen few more earnest, noble, and sincere "prophets," but not before warning its readers that Muhammad's mind "contained the strangest mixture of right and wrong, of truth and error."[150] And W. H. T. Gairdner in 1909 reflected too on the dark and light side of Muhammad's character: "Spirit and flesh, gold and clay, higher-than and lower-than average human nature – such is the strange double phenomenon that Mohammed presents to us all through; and with him, the religion he founded, the Book he left, the history he caused, the organisation he initiated."[151]

However that may be, there was a general consensus of opinion among Victorian writers that Muhammad, for all his faults, had been a boon to the Arabs, and to the East in general. He had after all abolished idolatry and polytheism. As William Taylor declared in 1834, "Let the Arabian prophet be called Heresiarch and Imposter; – yes, but a Reformer too. He kindled... an extraordinary abhorrence of idol worship, and actually cleansed the plains of Asia from the long settled impurities of polytheism."[152] To *The Foreign Quarterly Review* in 1840, his ethical injunctions were well suited to reform the perverted feelings of his countrymen.[153] Even Samuel Green saw him as a man of superior character considerably in advance of the age in which he lived, though he added the qualification that the rude and barbarous age which made him by comparison great "might have left him little more than a common man in the cultivated climes of Europe."[154] *The Prospective Review* for 1846 found him the channel of un-numbered blessings to his country. He denounced moral evil, enjoined humanity, mercy, humility, sincerity, and chastity in word and act, and asserted the resurrection of the dead and judgement in the world to come. "If these doctrines," it concluded, "are but a feeble echo of the Jewish and Christian revelations, yet, as Judaism and Christianity... had both failed in silencing Heathenism, we should, at least, rejoice that, through him, the cry of There is no god but God! did at length cast down the idols for ever."[155] In that most widely

---

149 Irving, *Life of Mahomet*, p. 240.
150 *Chamber's Encyclopaedia*, 1874, vi. 504.
151 Gairdner, *The Reproach of Islam*, p. 67.
152 Taylor, *The History of Mohammedanism*, p. 166.
153 See *The Foreign Quarterly Review*, 1840, p. 13.
154 Green, *The Life of Mahomet*, p. 215.
155 *The Prospective Review*, 1846, p. 173; see also *Dublin University Magazine*, 1876, p. 145; Barthélemy Saint-Hilarie, *Mahomet et le Coran*, p. 82.

read of books about Islam in Africa, *The Martyrdom of Man*, Winwood Reade was undoubtedly echoing the sentiments of many Victorians:

> Instead of repining that Mahomet did
> no more, we have reason to be
> astonished that he did so much. His
> career is the best example that can be
> given of the influence of the Individual
> in human history. That single man
> created the glory of his nation
> and spread his language over half the earth.[156]

But Muhammad was not merely a prime example of the "great man" in history, he was also an ideal Victorian. The Victorians' cataloguing of his virtues is a reflection of their own image of the ideal man projected onto the Prophet. For there was a clear resemblance between the Victorian image of the noble Arab and the Victorian concept of a gentleman. Muhammad as the noble Arab was also Muhammad the English gentleman, for that which was applauded in the Prophet typified ideas of Victorian gentlemanliness: simplicity of life, boundless liberality, kindness and affability to all, gentleness to inferiors, children, and animals, delicate consideration for the comfort and feelings of others, modesty, gentle speech, decisiveness in judgement, courageousness in thought and action. These were the attributes which, when seen as characteristic of Muhammad, led his character to be seen as a "singularly noble and beautiful one,"[157] and him to be viewed as "all great things in one,"[158] as "one of the greatest ever sent on earth,"[159] and as one to whom may be accorded "the largest amount of credit for every excellent human quality that a man may possess out of the pale of Christian discipleship."[160] For many, in spite of his human failings, as manly, chivalrous, benevolent, morally and physically courageous, he was a Carlylean hero, noble Arab, and an ideal Victorian.[161]

---

156 Reade, *The Martyrdom of Man*, pp. 268–9.
157 Davies, "Mohammed," p. 251.
158 Smith, *Mohammed and Mohammedanism*, p. 287.
159 *Dublin University Magazine*, 1873, p. 473.
160 *The Eclectic Magazine*, 1850, p. 49.
161 On manliness in Victorian literature, see Vance, *The Sinews of the Spirit*.

Epilogue

Thus, during the course of the nineteenth century, new images of Muhammad arose, accompanied by new attitudes to the religion instituted by him. Many of the ancient images persisted; Muhammad remained heretic, Anti-christ, ambitious imposter, profligate politician. But these were tempered by new images of the Prophet as sincere hero, noble Arab, and even true prophet of God.

The reasons for the change were, as we have seen, many. Increased data about Muhammad and the origins of Islam made early stereotypes ineffective. The demise of Christian apocalypticism and the rise of secular historical method created the Muhammad of history, relagating to the shadows the Muhammad of Christian legend. The Victorian penchant for great men coupled with the Western fascination for an exotic East engendered a sympathetic environment for the rehabilitation of Muhammad and Islam. And the rise of Western power over Islam made for a context in which the Prophet and his religion could be treated benevolently, even while it continued to encourage and support criticism of its modern manifestations.

The Victorian period in particular thus generated images of Muhammad and Islam which made it increasingly difficult to sustain those inherited from earlier periods, although they continued throughout the period, and do so today still. Old fears and ancient prejudices have recently reemerged in contemporary discourse, sympathy for, even admiration of an ideal, "essential" Islam have remained. That such conflicting images of Islam shall continue is perhaps inevitable while the notion of "Islam" remains a central feature of our classifying of other cultures. On what the continuation of such images of Islam may mean for the future, we can only speculate. At the very least, it is hoped that this study will make us more self-conscious in our interpreting and imagining both Islam and other religious traditions.

Bibliography

Anon., *Four Treatises Concerning the Doctrine, Discipline and Worship of the Mahometans*, London: J. Darby, 1712.
Anon., *Here after followeth a lytell Treatise agaynst Mahumet and his cursed Sect*, London: n.p., 1530.
Anon., *Life and Actions of Mahomet, the Famous Oriental Imposter*, London: J. Lee, 1815.
Anon., *Life of Mahomet*, London: Baldwin and Cradock, 1829.
Anon., *Life of Mohammad*, Bombay: American Mission Press, 1851.
Anon., *Mahomet's Mission*, London: James Nisbet and Co., 1855.
Anon., *Reflections on Mohammedism and the Conduct of Mohammed*, London: J. Roberts, 1735.
Anon., *The History of Mahomet, The Great Imposter*, Falkirk: T. Johnston, 1821.
Anon., *The Life of Mahomet; or, the History of that Imposture, which was begun, carried on, and finally established by him in Arabia*, London: W. Hallgarth, 1799.
Anon., *The Life of Mohammed*, London: The Religious Tract Society, 1847.
Anon., *The Morality of the East; Extracted from the Koran of Mohammed*, London: W. Nicoll, 1766.
Addison, Lancelot, *The Life and Death of Mahumed, the Author of the Turkish Religion*, London: William Crooke, 1679.
Akehurst, George, *Imposture instanced in the Life of Mahomet*, London: Wertheim, Macintosh, and Hunt, 1859.
Alcock, Nathan and Thomas, *The Rise of Mahomet, Accounted for on Natural and Civil Principles*, London: G. Sael, 1796.
Ali, Muhsin J., *Scheherazade in England*, Washington: Three Continents Press, 1981.
Amos, *The New but True Life of the Carpenter*, Bristol: John Wright, 1903.
Andrae, Tor, *Mohammed: The Man and His Faith*, London: Allen and Unwin, 1956.
Arberry, Arthur J., *The Koran Interpreted*, 2 vols., London: Allen and Unwin, 1955.
Arnold, Matthew, *Essays in Criticism*, London: Macmillan, 1985.
Arnold, Thomas W., *The Preaching of Islam: A History of the Propagation of the Muslim Faith*, Westminster: Archibald Constable and Co., 1896.
Ayoub, Mahmoud, *The Qur'an and its Interpreters*, Albany: SUNY Press, 1984.

Babington, Churchill (ed.), *Polychronicon Ranulphi Higden Monachi Cestrenis*, London: Longman, Green, etc., 1876.
Badger, George P., "Mohammed and Mohammedanism," *The Contemporary Review* 26 (1875), 87–102.
Barthélemy Saint-Hilaire, Jules, *Mahomet et le Coran*, Paris: Didier et Cie., 1865.
Bayle, Pierre, *An Historical and Critical Dictionary*, 4 vols., London: Hunt and Clark, 1826.
Bedwell, William, *Mohammedis Imposturae: that is, a Discovery of the Manifold Forgeries, Falshoods, and horrible Impieties of the blasphemous Seducer Mohammed*, London: Richard Field, 1615.
Anon., "Mahommedanism: Its Rise and Present Progress," *Bentley's Miscellany* 27 (1850), 597–9.
Beverley, Robert M., *A Letter to Godfrey Higgins in Answer to his "Apology for the Life and Character of Mohammed,"* no place; Beverley, 1829.

Biddulph, William, *The Travels of Certaine Englishmen into Africa, Asia*, etc., London: W. Aspley, 1609.
Blunt, Henry, *A Voyage into the Levant*, London: Andrew Crook, 1664.
Blunt, Wilfrid S., *The Future of Islam*, London: Kegan Paul, Trench, and Co., 1882.
Blyden, Edward W., *Christianity, Islam and the Negro Race*, London: Whittingham and Co., 1887.
Boemus, Joannes, *The Fardle of Facions*, London: Kingston and Sutton, 1555.
Bosworth, C. Edmund, "Dramatisation of the prophet Muhammad's life: Henri de Bornier's Mahomet," *Numen* 17 (1970), 105–17.
Bosworth, C. Edmund, "The Prophet Vindicated: A Restoration Treatise on Islam and Muhammad," *Religion* 6 (1976), 1–12.
Boulainvilliers, Henri, *The Life of Mahomet*, London: W. Hinchliffe, 1731.
Brerewood, Edward, *Enquiries Touching the Diversity of Languages and Religions, through the Chief Parts of the World*, London: Samuel Mearne etc., 1674.
Anon., "Mahomet," *British Quarterly Review* 55 (1872), 101–35.
Browne, G. Latham, *Biography: The Aera of Mahomet, A.D. 527 to 629*, London: S.P.C.K., 1856.
Buckle, Henry, *The Beggar or the Soldier: Gautama or Mahomet*, Clifton: J. Baker and Sons, 1903.
Bush, George, *The Life of Mohammed*, New York: Harper and Bros., 1844.

Carlyle, Thomas, *On Heroes, Hero-Worship and the Heroic in History*, London: Chapman and Hall, 1907.
Casaubon, Meric, *A Treatise Concerning Enthusiasme*, London: Tho. Johnson, 1655.
Chadwick, Owen, *The Secularization of the European Mind in the Nineteenth Century*, Cambridge: Cambridge University Press, 1975.
Chamber's Encyclopaedia, London: Chambers, 1874.
Chew, Samuel C., *The Crescent and the Rose: Islam and England During the Renaissance*, New York: Octagon Books, 1965.
Anon., Review of G. Weil, *The Bible, The Koran, and the Talmud*, London: Longman and Co., 1846, *The Christian Remembrancer* 11 (1846), 435–54.
Anon., "Mahometanism," *The Christian Remembrancer* 29 (1855), 83–154.
Cludius, Herman H., *Muhammeds Religion*, Altona: Hammerich, 1809.
Anon., "Mahomet," *Colburn's New Monthly Magazine* 126 (1868), 192–202.
Coryat, Thomas, *Mr. Thomas Coriat to his Friends in England sendeth Greeting*, London: I.R., 1618.
Cyclopaedia, London: D. Midwinter et al., 1738.

Daniel, Norman, *Islam and the West: The Making of an Image*, Edinburgh: The University Press, 1960.
Daniel, Norman, *Islam, Europe and Empire*, Edinburgh: Edinburgh University Press, 1966.
Davies, J. Llewelyn, "Mohammed and his Religion," *Good Words* 19 (1878), 247–52, 326–32.
Dods, Marcus, *Mohammed, Buddha, and Christ*, London: Hodder and Stoughton, 1878.
Döllinger, Johannes, *Muhammeds Religion nach ihrer inneren Entwicklung und ihrem Einflusse auf das Leben der Völker*, München: Carl Wolf'sche Buchdruckerei, 1838.
Anon., "Döllinger on the Mohammedan Religion," *The Dublin Review* 7 (1839), 98–121.

Anon., "Islam," *The Dublin Review* 30 (1878), 398–427.
Anon., "Mohammed, and His Place in Universal History," *Dublin University Magazine* 81 (1873), 460–80.
Anon., "The Founder of Islam," *Dublin University Magazine* 88 (1876), 129–45.
Du Ryer, André, *The Alcoran of Mahomet*, London: n.p., 1649.

East, W. Quartermaine, *The Last Days of Great Men: Cromwell, Napoleon, Mahomet*, London: Sampson, Low, Marston, and Co., 1903.
Anon., "Mahomet and the Koran," *The Eclectic Magazine* 21 (1850), 36–56.
Anon., "Life and Times of Mohammed," *The Eclectic Magazine* 45 (1858), 456–70.
Anon., "The Great Arabian," *The Eclectic Magazine* 55 (1862), 27–36, 210–19.
The Edinburgh Encyclopaedia, Edinburgh: Blackwood, 1830.
Anon., review of G. Miller, *Lectures*, and C. Forster, *Mahometanism Unveiled*, *The Edinburgh Review*, 50 (1829–30), 287–344.
Anon., "Mahomet," *The Edinburgh Review* 124 (1866), 1–50.
Encyclopaedia Britannica, Edinburgh: A. Bell and C. Macfarquhar, 1771.
Encyclopaedia Britannica, Edinburgh: A. Bell and C. Macfarquhar, 1797.
Encyclopaedia Britannica, Edinburgh: Constable and Co., 1810.
Encyclopaedia Britannica, Edinburgh: Constable and Co., 1817.
Encyclopaedia Britannica, Edinburgh: Constable and Co., 1823.
The Encyclopaedia Britannica, Edinburgh: A. and C. Black, 1842.
The Encyclopaedia Britannica, Edinburgh: A. and C. Black, 1853–60.
The Encyclopaedia Edinensis, Edinburgh: John Anderson, 1827.
Encyclopaedia Metropolitana, London: B. Fellowes, etc., 1845.
The Encyclopaedia of Islam, Leiden: Brill, 1960.
Encyclopaedia Perthensis, Edinburgh: John Brown, 1816.
The English Encyclopaedia, London: G. Kearsley, 1802.
Anon., "Mohammed and Mohammedanism," *The Foreign Quarterly Review* 12 (1833), 192–208.
Anon., "Views and Objects of Mahomet in the Composition of the Koran," *The Foreign Quarterly Review* 24 (1840), 1–25.

Forster, Charles, *Mahometanism Unveiled*, 2 vols. London: J. Duncan and J. Cochran, 1829.
Freeman, Edward A., *The History and Conquest of the Saracens*, Oxford: John Henry and James Parker, 1856.
Futrell, Michael, "Dostoyevsky and Islam (and Chokan Valikhanov)," *The Slavonic and East European Review* 57 (1979), 16–31.

Gagnier, Jean, *Islam Abu'l-Feda de vita et rebus gestis Mohammedis*, Oxonia, 1723.
Gairdner, William H. T., *The Reproach of Islam*, London: Church Missionary Society, 1909.
Gay, Peter, *The Bourgeois Experience: Victoria to Freud*, New York: Oxford University Press, 1984.
Gibbon, Edward, *The History of the Decline and Fall of the Roman Empire*, 3 vols., London: Alexander Murray and Son, 1869.
Glacken, Clarence J., *Traces on the Rhodian Shore*, Berkeley: University of California Press, 1867.

Goldziher, Ignaz, *Introduction to Islamic Theology and Law*, Princeton: Princeton University Press, 1981.
Grant, George M., *The Religions of the World*, London: A. and C. Black, 1895.
Green, Samuel, *The Life of Mahomet, Founder of the Religion of Islam, and of the Empire of the Saracens*, London: Tegg, 1840.

Hardwick, Charles, *Christ and other Masters*, London: Macmillan, 1875.
Anon., "Mahomet," *Harper's New Monthly Magazine* 55 (1877), 402–12.
D'Herbelot, Bartholomaeo, *Bibliothèque orientale, ou Dictionnaire universel contenant tout ce qui fait connaître les peuples de l'Orient*, The Hague: Neaulme and van Daalen, 1777.
Herbert, Thomas, *Some Years Travels into Divers parts of Africa and Asia the Great*, London: Andrew Crook, 1665.
Heylyn, Peter, *Cosmographie: In Four Bookes*, London: Henry Seile, 1652.
Higgins, Godfrey, *An Apology for the Life and Character of the Celebrated Prophet of Arabia, called Mohamed, or The Illustrious*, London: Rowland Hunter, etc., 1829.
Holland, Edith, *The Story of Mohammed*, London: Harrap, 1914.
Holt, Peter M., "The Study of Arabic Historians in seventeenth century England: The background and work of Edward Pococke," *Bulletin of the School of Oriental and African Studies*, 19 (1957), 444–55.
Holt, Peter M., and Lewis, Bernard (eds.), *Historians of the Middle East*, London: Oxford University Press, 1962.
Anon., "Asceticism amongst Mahometan Nations," *Home and Foreign Review* 4 (1864), 553–76.
Houghton, Walter E., *The Victorian Frame of Mind, 1830–1870*, New Haven: Yale University Press, 1957.
Howden, James C., "The Religious Sentiment in Epileptics," *The Journal of Mental Science* 18 (1873), 482–97.

Irving, Washington, *Life of Mahomet*, London: J. M. Dent and Sons, 1920.

Jenkin, Robert, *The Reasonableness and Certainty of the Christian Religion*, London: P. B. and R. Wellington, 1700.
Johnstone, P. de Lacy, *Muhammad and His Power*, Edinburgh: T. and T. Clark, 1901.

Kaplan, Fred, *Thomas Carlyle: A Biography*, Cambridge: Cambridge University Press, 1983.
Kennedy, Vans, "Remarks on the Character of Muhammed," *Transactions of the Royal Asiatic Society of Bombay* 3 (1823), 398–448.
Knolles, Richard, *The Turkish History*, London: Th. Bassett, 1687.
Knox, Ronald A., *Enthusiasm*, Oxford: Clarendon, 1950.
Koelle, Sigismund W., *Mohammed and Mohammedanism Critically Considered*, London: Rivingtons, 1889.

Lane-Poole, Stanley, *Studies in a Mosque*, London: W. H. Allen and Co., 1883.
Lang, Bernhard, "The Sexual Life of the Saints," Religion 17 (1987), 149–71.
Le Mahieu, D. L., *The Mind of William Paley*, Lincoln: University of Nebraska Press, 1976.

Letts, Malcolm, *Mandeville's Travels: Text and Translations*, 2 vols., London: Hakluyt, 1953.
Lithgow, William, *A Most Delectable and True Discourse*, London: Thomas Archer, 1614.

Manuel, Frank E., *The Changing of the Gods*, Hanover: University Press of New England, 1983.
Marcus, Steven, *The Other Victorians*, London: Corgi, 1969.
Margoliouth, David S., *Mohammed and the Rise of Islam*, New York: G. P. Putnam's Sons, 1905.
Maurice Frederick D., *The Religions of the World and their Relation to Christianity*, London: John W. Parker, 1847.
Menezes, J. L., *The Life and Religion of Mahommed the Prophet of Arabia*, London: Sands and Co., 1911.
Metlitzki, Dorothee, *The Matter of Araby in Medieval England*, New Haven: Yale University Press, 1977.
Mildert, William van, *An Historical View of the Rise and Progress of Infidelity*, 2 vols., London: F. C. and J. Rivington, 1820.
Miller, George, *Lectures on the Philosophy of Modern History*, 8 vols., Dublin: J. Murray, 1816–28.
Miller, James, *Mahomet the Imposter: A Tragedy*, London: J. Watts, 1744.
Mills, Charles, *An History of Muhammedanism*, London: Black, Kingsbury, Parbury, and Allen, 1818.
Milman, Henry Hart, *History of Latin Christianity*, 6 vols., London: John Murray, 1854–5.
Miscellanea Aurea: or the Golden Medley, London: A. Bettesworth and J. Pemberton, 1720.
Moehler, Johann A., *On the Relation of Islam to the Gospel*, Calcutta: Ostell and Lepage, 1847.
Morgan, Joseph, *Mahometism Fully Explained*, 2 vols., London: W. Mears, 1723.
Muenster, Sebastian, *A Brief Collection... Gathered out of the Cosmographye of Sebastian Munster*, London: T. Marshe, 1572.
Muir, William, "Islam and Christianity," *The Leisure Hour* (1885), 133–4.
Muir, William, *The Life of Moḥammad from Original Sources*, Edinburgh, John Grant, 1923.
Muir, William, *The Mohammedan Controversy*, Edinburgh: T. and T. Clark, 1897.

Nash, Geoffrey, "Thomas Carlyle and Islam," *World Order* 19 (1984–5), 9–22.
Nasr, Seyyed H., *Ideals and Realities of Islam*, London: Allen and Unwin, 1966.
The National Cyclopaedia of Useful Knowledge, London: Charles Knight, 1847–51.
Anon., "Mohammed and His Institutions," *The National Quarterly Review*, 33 (1876), 201–28.
Anon., "Mahomet," *National Review* 7 (1858), 137–60.
Anon., "The Great Arabian," *National Review* 13 (1861), 309–40.
Newman, John H., *Lectures on the History of the Turks in its Relation to Christianity*, Dublin: James Duffy, 1854.
Anon., "The Biographers of Mohammad," *The New Quarterly Review* 2 (1853) 200–5.
Nöldeke, Theodor, *Das Leben Muhammeds*, Hannover: Carl Rümpler, 1863.
Anon., "Mahometanism in the East and West," *The North British Review* 23 (1855), 449–80.

Ockley, Simon, *The History of the Saracens*, London: Henry G. Bohn, 1847.
Osborn, Robert D., *Islam under the Arabs*, London: Longmans, Green, and Co., 1876.
Owen, Alfred A., "Polygamy and Deism," *The Journal of English and Germanic Philology*, 48 (1949), 343–60.

Pailin, David A., *Attitudes to Other Religions: Comparative Religion in seventeenth and eighteenth century Britain*, Manchester: Manchester University Press, 1984.
Paley, William, *The Works*, Edinburgh: Peter Brown and Thomas Nelson, 1831.
Palgrave, William G., *Narrative of a Year's Journey Through Central and Eastern Arabia*, 2 vols., London: Macmillan, 1865.
Palmer, Edward H., *The Qur'ān*, Oxford: Clarendon Press, 1900.
Pantologia, London: G. Kearsley, etc., 1813.
The Penny Cyclopaedia, London: Charles Knight and Co., 1833.
Pfander, C. G., *Remarks on the Nature of Muhammadanism*, Calcutta: Baptist Mission Press, 1840.
Pitts, Joseph, *A True and Faithful Account of the Religion and Manners of the Mohammetans*, Exeter: P. Bishop and E. Score, 1704.
Porteus, Beilby, *A Summary of the Principal Evidences for the Trutz and Divine Origin of the Christian Revelation*, London: T. Cadell, etc., 1800.
Power, Edmond, *The Religion of the Korān*, London: Catholic Truth Society, 1909.
Prideaux, Humphrey, *The True Nature of Imposture Fully Displayed in the Life of Mahomet*, London: William Rogers, 1697.
Anon., "The Life and Doctrine of Mohammed the Prophet, drawn from Manuscript sources and the Koran," *The Prospective Review* 2 (1846), 159–73.
Anon., "Islam," *The Quarterly Review* 127 (1869), 293–353.
Anon., review of R. B. Smith, *Mohammed and Mohammedanism*, *The Quarterly Review* 143 (1877), 205–37.

Raleigh, Walter, *The Life and Death of Mahomet*, London: Daniel Frére, 1637.
Reade, Winwood, *The Martyrdom of Man*, London: Kegan Paul, Trench, Trübner and Co., 1896.
Reland, Adrian, "Of the Mahometan Religion," *Four Treatises*.
Renan, Ernst, *Studies of Religious History*, London: William Heinemann, 1893.
Reventlow, Henning Graf, *The Authority of the Bible and the Rise of the Modern World*, Philadelphia: Fortress Press, 1985.
Rodinson, Maxime, "The Life of Muhammad and the sociological Problem of the Beginnings of Islam," *Diogenes* 20 (1957), 28–51.
Roebuck John, *Life of Mahomet*, London: Baldwin and Cradock, 1833.
Ross, Alexander, *Pansebeia: or, A View of all Religions in the World*, London: John Williams, 1683.
Rowell, Geoffrey, *Hell and the Victorians*, Oxford: Clarendon 1974.

Said, Edward, *Orientalism*, London: Routledge and Kegan Paul, 1978.
Said, Edward, *The World, the Text, and the Critic*, Cambridge, Massachusetts: Harvard University Press, 1983.
Sale, George, *The Koran; commonly called, the Alcoran of Mohammed*, London: Charles Daly, 1836.
Sandys, George, *Sandys Travailes*, London: R. and W. Leybourn, 1608.

Sandys, George, *Sandys Travels*, London: John Williams Junior, 1673.
Schimmel, Annemarie, *And Muhammad is His Messenger*, Chapel Hill: The University of North Carolina Press, 1985.
Sime, William, *History of Mohammed and his Successors*, Edinburgh: William Oliphant and Son, 1837.
Sismondi, Jean C. L. de, *A History of the Fall of the Roman Empire*, 2 vols., London: Longman, Brown, Green and Longmans, 1834.
Smith, Byron, P., *Islam in English Literature*, New York: Caravan Books, 1977.
Smith, George A., *Mohammedanism and Christianity*, London: Stockwell, 1908.
Smith, Henrie, *Gods Arrovve against Atheists*, London: W. Bailey, 1593.
Smith, R. Bosworth, *Mohammed and Mohammedanism*, London: John Murray, 1889.
Smith, Thomas, *Remarks Upon the Manners, Religion, and Government of the Turks*, London: Moses Pitt, 1678.
Sprenger, Aloys, *Das Leben und die Lehre des Moḥammed*, 3 vols., Berlin: Nicolai'sche Verlagsbuchhandlung, 1861–5.
Sprenger, Aloys, *Mohammed und der Koran. Eine psychologische Studie*, Hamburg: Verlagsanstalt und Druckerei A.-G., 1889.
Sprenger, Aloys, *The Life of Mohammed from Original Sources*, Allahabad: Presbyterian Mission Press, 1851.
Stephens, William R. W., *Christianity and Islam*, London: Richard Bentley and Son, 1877.
Stubbe, Henry, *An Account of the Rise and Progress of Mahometanism with the Life of Mahomet*, London: Luzac and Co., 1911.

Taylor, Isaac, *Fanaticism*, New York: Jonathan Leavitt, 1834.
Taylor, William Cooke, *The History of Mohammedanism and its Sects*, London: John W. Parker, 1834.
Temkin, Owsei, *The Falling Sickness*, Baltimore: The Johns Hopkins Press, 1971.
Thompson, T. Perronet, "Arabs and Persians," *Westminster Review* 6 (1826), 202–48.
Tidrick, Kathryn, *Heart-beguiling Araby*, Cambridge: Cambridge University Press, 1981.
Tillotson, John (ed.), *The Works of the Learned Isaac Barrow*, 3 vols., London: Brabazon Aylmer, 1700.
Townsend, Meredith, *Mahommed: "The Great Arabian,"* London: Constable and Co., 1912.
Trowbridge, T. C., "Mohammedanism and the Ottoman Turks," *The British Quarterly Review* 75 (1882) 273–94.
Turner, Bryan S., "Orientalism, Islam and Capitalism," *Social Compass* 25 (1978), 371–94.
Turtledove, Harry, *The Chronicle of Theophanes*, Philadelphia: University of Pennsylvania Press, 1982.

Upham, Edward, *History of the Ottoman Empire*, 2 vols., Edinburgh: Constable and Co., 1829.
Urquhart, David, *The Spirit of the East, illustrated in a Journal of Travels through Roumeli during an Eventful Period*, 2 vols., London: Henry Colburn, 1838.

Vance, Norman, *The Sinews of the Spirit*, Cambridge: Cambridge University Press, 1985.
Voltaire, François-Marie A., *Œuvres Complètes de Voltaire*, Paris: E. A. Lequien, 1820–6.

Watt, Ian, *The Rise of the Novel*, Harmondsworth: Penguin, 1963.
Watt, W. Montgomery, *Bell's Introduction to the Qur'ān*, Edinburgh: Edinburgh University Press, 1970.

Watt, W. Montgomery, "Carlyle on Muhammad," *The Hibbert Journal* 53 (1954–5), 247–54.
Weil, Gustav, *Mohammed der Prophet, sein Leben und seine Lehre*, Stuttgart: J. B. Metzler, 1843.
Whetstones, George, *The English Myrror*, London: G. Seton, 1586.
White, Joseph, *Sermons Preached before the University of Oxford in the year 1784*, Dublin: John Exshaw and Luke White, 1785.
Widengren, Geo, *Muḥammad, the Apostle of God, and his Ascension*, Uppsala: Lundequistska bokhandeln, 1955.
Williams, George H., "Erasmus and the Reformers on Non-Christian Religions and *Salus Extra Ecclesiam*," Theodore K. Raab and Jerrold E. Seigel (eds.), *Action and Conviction in Early Modern Europe*, Princeton: Princeton University Press, 1969, pp. 319–70.
Williamson, David, *Reflections on the Four Principal Religions, which have obtained in the World*, 2 vols., London: John Richardson, 1824.
Wollheim, Richard (ed.), *Hume on Religion*, London: Collins, 1963.
Wybarne, Joseph, *The New Age of Old Names*, London: W. Barrett and H. Fetherstone, 1609.

Index

Abdella (Abdollah) 66–67
Abu'l-Feda 13, 14, 89, 90
Addison, Lancelot 16, 20 n, 34 n, 57, 63 n
Akehurst, George 10, 35, 36 n, 69
Alcock, Nathan 17, 46
Alcock, Thomas 34, 68
Alfonsi, Petrus 66
Ali, Muhsin 46 n
Andrae, Tor 28 n
Antichrist, Muhammad as the 1, 6–10 *passim*
Apocalyptic, Christian 5, 7, 8, 31, 87
Arabian Nights, The 3, 46–47
Arberry, Arthur 74
Arminius, Jacob, Muhammad and 44
Arnold, Matthew, 5 nAugustine of Hippo, St. Muhammad and 44

Babington, Churchill 22 n, 57 n
Badger, George 39 n, 62 n, 76 n, 77, 82 n, 86 n
Bahira, (Sergius) 66–67, 68
Barthélemy Saint-Hilaire, Jules 9, 19, 31, 87, 91, 92 n
Bayle, Pierre 11, 50, 63 n
Beauvais, Vincent of 21–22
Beverly, Robert 14, 57
Biddulph, William 23, 49, 66
Blunt, Henry 46, 49 n, 86 n
Blyden, Edward 37 n, 77 n, 84, 86 n
Bosworth, C. E. 33 n
Boulainvilliers, Henri 14–15, 51, 59, 68, 79, 81
British Monarch, Islam and the 39–40
Browne, G. Latham 25, 30, 36 n
Buckle, Henry 29 n
Buddha, the, Muhammad and 6, 35, 78, 91
Bush, George 28 n
Butler, Bishop Joseph 50

Calvin, John, Muhammad and 44
Carlyle, Thomas 3, 4, 6, 15, 19, 20, 40, 41, 47, 48, 49, 62, 75, 76, 77, 78, 89, 93
Casaubon, Meric 16

Chadwick, Owen 52
Chew, Samuel 66 n, 73
Clarke, Samuel 50
Cludius, H. H. 17
Confucius, Muhammad and 78
Coryat, Thomas 67, 69
Cromwell, Oliver, Muhammad and 20

Daniel, Norman ix, 7 n, 36 n, 38, 45 n, 48 n, 50, 56, 58, 59 n, 60 n, 86 n
Davies, J. Llewelyn 31 n, 62 n, 93 n
Deutsch, Eliot 6 n
Dods, Marcus 30 n, 38, 44 n, 49, 62 n
Döllinger, Johannes 61 n, 84
Dostoievski, Feodor 55

East, W. Quartermaine 20, 77, 90 n
Eschatology, Christian, Islam and 48–49

Forster, Charles 5, 8, 71, 79 n, 87
Freeman, Edward 4, 32, 62 n, 80, 82–83, 86 n
Futrell, Michael 55

Gabriel, the Archangel 1, 21, 22, 23, 24, 25, 65
Gagnier, Jean 13, 14, 23, 89
Gairdner, William 83, 84, 87 n, 90 n, 92
Galland, Antoine (author of *The Arabian Nights*) 46
Gay, Peter 61 n
Gibbon, Edward 14, 23, 24, 28, 29, 30, 48, 74, 75
Glacken, Clarence 59 n, 60 n
Goethe, J. W. von 6, 47
Goldhizer, Ignaz 29 n
Grant, George 29 n, 41 n, 43 n, 62, 74 n, 79, 83 n
Green, Samuel 28 n, 47, 69 n, 71, 92
Grotius, Hugo 69

D'Herbelot, Bartholomaeo 6, 11, 13
Herbert, Thomas 7, 45, 56 n, 67, 69, 77 n
Herder, J. G. von 3

Index

Heylyn, Peter 9, 23, 57 n, 67, 69, 88 n
Higden, Ranulph 22
Higgins, Godfrey 13, 14, 40, 81
Hijra, the (journey to Medina) 1
Historical-critical scholarship, Islam and 1, 5, 6, 13–14, 52, 94
Holland, Edith 35, 39–40, 90 n
Holt, Peter 48, 70 n
Hottinger, J. H. 13, 14
Houghton, Walter 78 n
Howden, James 25, 26 n
Hume, David 50, 51, 59

Irving, Washington 5, 18, 19, 24, 31, 56, 77, 89, 91

Jenkin, Robert 56
John of Antioch 66
Johnstone, de Lacy 8, 29 n, 47, 62 n, 83 n, 90 n

Kennedy, Vans 17, 18, 30, 48 n
Khadija, (wife of Muhammad) 1, 21, 22, 45–46, 57–58; death of 58; *see also* Polygamy, Women
Knolles, Richard 67
Koelle, S. W. 4, 5, 20, 27, 29 n, 35 n, 57, 58 n, 69, 86 n

Lane-Poole, Stanley 25, 43 n, 58 n, 62–63, 74, 76 n, 86, 90 n
Lang, Bernard 47 n
Le Mahieu, D. L. 50 n
Lithgow, William 22, 67
Locke, John 50
Long, Dr. (Master of Pembroke) 48 n, 90

Mandeville, John 22
Manuel, Frank 46 n
Marcus, Steven 47
Margoliouth, David 23, 24, 90 n
Marraci, Ludovico 13, 19, 74
Maurice, Frederick D. 5, 6 n, 36, 72
Metlitzki, Dorothee 66 n
Mildert, William van, (Bishop of Llandaff) 51, 69, 86 n
Mill, John Stuart 61

Miller, George 80, 84–85, 97
Miller, James 33
Mills, Charles 17, 28, 43, 47 n, 55, 75 n, 80
Milman, Henry H. 28, 29, 32, 47, 71, 81
Missions, Protestant, Islam and 4, 36–41 *passim* 81
Moehler, J. 15, 19, 30, 39, 77, 86 n
Montesquieu, Baron de 60
Muenster, Sebastian 22, 66, 69, 88
Muir, William 6, 8, 9, 13 n, 19, 20, 31, 32, 37, 43, 45, 46, 55, 76, 83, 87 n, 89, 91

Nasr, Seyyed 35
Newmann, John Henry 87
Nöldeke, Theodor 6

Ockley, Simon 48, 54, 90
Omar, Mahumed Abdulla 12, 34, 37, 60, 67, 68
Osborne, Robert 29 n, 37 n, 43, 84
Owen, Alfred 59 n

Pailin, David 37 n, 50
Paley, William 29 n, 36 n, 42 n, 50 60
Palgrave, William 43, 57 n, 83
Palmer, Edward 27, 30 n, 62, 76 n, 80 n, 90
Pelagius, Muhammad and 44
Percival, Caussin de 19, 91
Pfander, C. G. 47 n, 50 n
Pitts, Joseph (sailor) 57, 70
Plato, Muhammad and 78
Pococke, Edward 13, 14, 69, 70
Polygamy; Muhammad, Islam and 58–64 *passim*
Pope, the 5, 9, 10
Porteus, Beilby (Bishop of London) 36, 50, 60 n, 63, 70–71, 77
Power, Edmond 84
Prideaux, Humphrey 6, 9, 10, 11–12, 13, 14, 19, 22, 23, 24, 34, 35, 36, 37, 46, 53, 54, 59, 60, 63, 64, 67, 68, 70 n

Quran, the; Christian and Jewish influences on 65–73; translations of 73–78; (English) 8, 16, 22, 37, 65, 69, 73–78, 97, 100; (French) 8, 73; (Latin) 74; Western tastes and 73–78

Raleigh, Sir Walter 23, 67
Reade, Winwood 25, 31, 86, 93
Reland, Adrian 13, 48
Renan, Ernst 5, 30, 83, 91
Reventlow, H. Graf 52 n
Roebuck, John 5, 6, 54, 75, 85
Ross, Alexander 7–8, 65, 66, 67, 79 n
Rowell, Geoffrey 49 n
Ryer, André du 8, 22 n, 65 n, 69 n, 73, 77 n

Sa'd, Ibn 89
Said, Edward ix 2, 5 n, 11, 75 n
Sale, George 13, 14, 16–17, 23, 37, 54, 59, 68, 74, 75, 76, 90
Sandys, George 23, 66, 67 n, 69, 88
Satan, Muhammad and 3, 6, 7–10, 11, 20, 51, 66, 68, 86
Schimmel, Annemarie 21, 29 n, 53 n, 58 n, 88–89
Schlegel, Friedrich 3
Schönlein, J. 26
Sergius, *see* Bahira
Sime, William 14, 35, 45, 54, 81
Sismondi, Jean de 29, 30 n, 42 n, 45, 62
Smith, Byron P. (20th cent) 23 n, 65 n
Smith, George Adam, (20th cent) 32, 83, 86 n
Smith, Henrie (16th cent) 57, 66, 69, 85 n
Smith, R. Bosworth (19th cent) 19, 20, 31, 39, 43–44, 52, 61, 62, 63, 72, 77, 81, 83 n, 85, 86, 87–88, 89, 93 n
Smith, Thomas, (17th cent) 42, 56, 67, 85 n
Sprenger, Aloys 6, 9, 26–27, 55, 56, 57 n, 91
Stephens, William 72 n
Stubbe, Henry 23, 40, 41, 48, 49, 51 n, 59, 67, 68, 70, 81, 88

Taylor, Isaac 38, 39

Taylor, William 71, 80 n, 82, 92
Temkin, Owsei 24, 55
Temperature, Sexuality and 59–60
Tennyson, Alfred Lord 47
Thackeray, William 44
Theophanes, (Byzantine historian) 21
Thompson, T. Perronet, (MP, FRS) 42–43, 48 n, 60, 74
Tidrick, Kathryn 46–47, 82
Tillotson, John 36 n, 85 n
Townsend, Meredith 43 n, 63
Trowbridge, T. C. 45, 57, 61, 62 n, 83
Turks 7, 42, 44, 83–85; alliance against Russia of the 4; as dissolute voluptuaries 44–49 *passim*; 56–64 *passim*
Turtledove, Harry 21, 45

Upham, Edward 71
Urquhart, David 61

Vance, Norman 93 n
Vitry, Jacques de 7
Voltaire, F.-M. A. 19, 33, 34, 35, 64

Waraqah (teacher of Muhammad) 66 n
Watt, Ian 59 n
Weil, Gustav 19, 24, 25, 91
Wesley, Charles 7
Whetstones, George 66
White, Joseph 13, 50, 58, 70, 80, 81
Widengren, Geo 53 n
Williamson, David 10 n, 71
Wollheim, Richard 50
Women, the state of; Muhammad, Islam and 56–64, 85; *see also* Polygamy, Khadija (wife of Muhammad)
Wybarne, Joseph 22, 69